THE STRUGGLE FOR AMERICA'S SOUL

THE STRUGGLE FOR AMERICA'S SOUL

Evangelicals, Liberals, and Secularism

Robert Wuthnow

WILLIAM B. EERDMANS PUBLISHING COMPANY
GRAND RAPIDS, MICHIGAN

Copyright © 1989 by Wm. B. Eerdmans Publishing Co.
255 Jefferson Ave. S.E., Grand Rapids, Mich. 49503

Library of Congress Cataloging-in-Publication Data

Wuthnow, Robert.
  The struggle for America's soul: evangelicals, liberals, and
secularism / Robert Wuthnow
        p.   cm.
    ISBN 0-8028-3669-0 — ISBN 0-8028-0469-1 (pbk.)
    1. United States—Church history—20th century.
    2. Evangelicalism—United States—History—20th century.
    3. Liberalism (Religion)—United States—History—20th century.
    4. Sociology, Christian—United States—History—20th century.
    I. Title.
BR517.W88   1989
277.3'0828—dc20   89-39340
                                                             CIP

Contents

Acknowledgments   vii

Prologue   ix

I • CONTOURS OF THE FAITH

    One   The Major Players   3

    Two   Old Fissures, New Fractures   19

    Three   Contested Terrain   39

    Four   Struggle in One Denomination   68

II • DYNAMICS OF THE SECULAR

    Five   Civil Privatism and the State   97

    Six   Paradox and Media   115

    Seven   Science and the Sacred   142

    Eight   The Costs of Marginality   158

Epilogue   177

Index   187

Acknowledgments

IN PREPARING THESE ESSAYS I incurred debts to a number of colleagues, students, clergy, and church people. It was very much their encouragement that convinced me of the importance of addressing these issues and their feedback that helped me refine the arguments. I developed most of these essays initially as public lectures and, although they have gone through many revisions, I have tried to retain some of their original style. I am especially grateful to the following institutions and individuals for providing me with these opportunities: Oberlin College, the Institute for Advanced Christian Studies, Wheaton College, Calvin College, Fairfield University, Emory University, Yale University, the University of Chicago, the Eastern Sociological Society, Gettysburg College, the University of Texas, the University of Notre Dame, Princeton Theological Seminary, Louisville Presbyterian Theological Seminary, the Williamsburg Charter Foundation, Mark Noll, Corwin Schmidt, Jay Dolan, Arthur Holmes, Frank Lechner, Quentin Schultze, Paul DiMaggio, Steven Tipton, Joel Carpenter, Jan Shipps, Wendy Griswold, John Mulder, Louis Weeks, Dorothy Bass, Lester Kurtz, and James Hunter.

Permission to reprint portions of the following was granted by the respective publishers: "Quid Obscurum: The Changing Terrain of Church-State Relations," in *Religion and American Politics*, ed. Mark Noll (Oxford: Oxford University Press, 1989); "Government Activity and Civil Privatism: Evidence from Voluntary Church Membership" (with Clifford Nass), *Journal for the Scientific Study of Religion* 27 (June 1988): 157-74; and "Science and the Sacred," in *The Sacred in a Secular Age,* ed. Phillip E. Hammond (Berkeley: University of California Press, 1985), pp. 187-203. Some of the material in several of the chapters is scheduled to appear in a revised form in various conference volumes still in preparation. I owe special thanks to George Marsden and Gail Ullman for comments on the manuscript, to Gary Lee at Eerdmans for editorial advice, and to Robert Lynn at the Lilly Endowment and John Wilson of Princeton University for research support.

Prologue

ONE RAINY AFTERNOON IN LATE SPRING a small group of students and faculty gathered on the Princeton campus. Their task was to advance in some way toward a better understanding of the relations between American religion and American society. Outside, the world was fairly bursting with fresh life responding to the rain's warm encouragement. Inside, the ambience seemed cold and dry. It was a day when new ideas would have to be lively indeed to compete with the creativity going on elsewhere of its own accord.

The group's topic for this day had been announced as "How to Respond to the Religious Right." A curious bystander might have wondered whether Norman Lear, the American Civil Liberties Union, or some other liberal movement had come to town. A more knowledgeable observer would probably have guessed that yet another tedious academic lecture was under way. But neither of these was the case.

The leader, a visiting professor from another university, opened the discussion this way: "A couple of years ago, I happened to be at a conference and a film was shown that really aroused my passions. It was a film about the dangers of the Religious Right. I was deeply moved. And yet, I haven't known quite what, as a teacher, I should do. Some of my friends tell me a professor's job is to profess, and so, if I feel passionately that the Religious Right is a threat to our society, I should say so. Others tell me a professor's job is to educate, not advocate. In their view, I should discuss the Religious Right with my students but keep my feelings about it to myself." With this brief introduction, he showed the film and asked us to discuss the quandary he had posed.

The film itself was fairly unsurprising to anyone familiar with the evening news and the lively discussion about the Religious Right that the media have promoted in recent years. One after another, the scenes moved from outrageous statements culled from the public appearances of Jerry Falwell and James Robison, to equally outrageous interview segments with Richard Viguerie and Paul Weyrich of the secular right, to maudlin accounts of heavy-handed school board decisions and frenzied shots of public book burnings—all modulated with the reasoned voice-over commentary of Burt Lancaster. In less than thirty minutes the film surveyed the Religious Right's views on democracy and theocracy, the behind-the-scenes technology and manipulation that were helping to advance their cause, and the ways in which right-wing leaders were conspiring to curb civil liberties for all, to restrict the honest airing of opinions, and even to promote child abuse and execute homosexuals. It was indeed a film that aroused the passions.

The discussion that ensued was scarcely less passionate than the film. One member of the group was outraged that the film seemed to be calling for a blatant campaign of censorship against the Religious Rig. at the same time that it piously pronounced judgment on anyone else who wanted to curb civil liberties. Another ventured that if a majority of the people decided to take freedom of speech out of the Constitution, they had the right to do so. Still another thought book burnings had to be tolerated as long as there were no laws against them, while another countered that book burnings were repugnant even if they were legal.

As the discussion progressed, additional issues—closer to the ones the leader had initially posed—came tumbling out. Should one assume that the film was an accurate portrayal of the Religious Right, or should it be regarded as an example of propaganda? To what extent was it desirable to focus discussions of this sort on questions of legality and constitutionality? Would doing so unduly restrict the possibilities for creative responses or even positive social change? Could one be content to consider alternative points of view about the Religious Right from students, letting them draw their own conclusions? Or was it better to confess one's own prejudices from the start? Did the answer to this question depend on the kind of class one was teaching? Were there dangers in being too relativistic and accepting about controversial issues, thereby allowing dangerous movements to prosper more than they should simply by being taken seriously? And was it enough to let the discussion rise to more abstract levels of intellectual generality? Or should a responsible approach also work back down the level of abstraction to bring intellectual insights to bear on more practical questions of public policy?

At the close of the discussion, the leader offered a modest proposal. He suggested that the answer to the question he had posed at the outset was to be found in the question itself. Or, more precisely, it was to be found in the process of questioning. He had deliberately structured the discussion so that we would discover that answer for ourselves. We had expressed our views, often with passion, but we had also listened. We had focused, not on the question of what to do about the Religious Right, but on what kind of discussion to have about it. In doing so, we had been forced to confront one another with the assumptions we were making and with the criteria on which we were willing to judge one another's arguments. The discussion turned out to be about the nature of discussion, a meta-discussion that offered glimpses into the process of discussion itself.

In choosing to recount this episode, I betray my own conclusion that it was a useful and insightful endeavor. Our discussion of the Religious Right exemplifies the predicament we face in American religion more generally. This is the problem of being true to our own religious convictions—holding them with passion—and yet knowing how to behave properly in public life, where we must interact with people who do not share our convictions.

Many discussions of how religion should, or should not, be treated as an element of public life in the United States suffer from a vague notion of how American society is organized. Like our group at Princeton University, sitting in a circle discussing our views about religion, the society at large seems to be a big circle—perhaps located somewhere in Washington, D.C.—with religious leaders and public officials all conferring in solemn tones.

But if this image might have applied in Jefferson's day, it clearly falls short of reality at the end of the twentieth century. It is equally inaccurate if we think only in terms of the courts or the mass media as circles in which public debate is located. It is clearly important to keep abreast of how the courts are deciding on issues that affect the religious life of the nation, and to consider whether the media are treating religion evenhandedly or in some way biasing the public's perception. But these considerations constitute more the tip of the iceberg—the part we can see—than the underlying structure that actually makes a difference.

In the next chapter, I have tried to present a novel—and hopefully more systematic—way of thinking about the social location that religion occupies in American society. If we are to understand the struggle for America's soul, we must begin by understanding who the major players in this struggle are. They are not the American Civil Liberties Union, the National Council of Churches, the Southern Baptist Convention, or other groups of similar prominence. I have tried to suggest the importance of placing religion within the context of the many thousands of other voluntary associations that some have begun to call the "third sector." Then it makes sense to ask how this sector is distinguished from the other major players that make up the first and second sectors of our society—government and private firms. It also makes sense to ask how changes in the political and economic sectors have affected the religious sphere in recent years, and how these changes are likely to continue shaping it in the near future. In short, where do the churches fit into American society?

Of course, this is only the first step. The struggle itself—at least the one I wish to try to understand—is taking place within the religious sphere itself. It is a struggle being waged between religious factions. Neither faction is monolithic, but on many issues in recent years, two clearly identifiable groups have lined up to wage spiritual warfare with each other. One side has styled itself the conservative wing of American religion. The other side has taken a liberal stance toward the issues that conservatives have championed. Who constitutes these two factions? How do they view each other? How have changes in our society over the past generation contributed to the conflict between them?

The struggle going on in American religion has roots in different views of the Bible, in different styles of moral reasoning, and even in different concepts of spirituality. These are important and as yet insufficiently understood. We do know, however, that the public life of the nation has been much affected in recent years by the turmoil in American religion. Indeed, it appears that both the major contestants have mobilized to fight social and political battles as much as to defend their distinctive views of the sacred. Suddenly, religion is playing an aggressive role in the public arena—a role that many in our society, and perhaps in our churches as well, had not expected and have had trouble explaining. Consequently, we hear much about the resurgence of religion, and we hear various accounts of why religion is flexing its muscles and trying to shape public debate. Unfortunately, some of these arguments are plainly wrong, and others need to be seriously qualified.

Sometimes it is easy to read accounts of the struggles going on in American religion in the newspaper, or to hear discussions of these struggles on television newscasts or talk shows, and to come away with the impression that the trouble is rather shallow. It is easy to conclude that religious conflict is the work of a few highly visible and highly motivated religious leaders, like some of the prominent television preachers, or that it is a brushfire being fanned by the media for the sake of keeping up their ratings.

Those at the helm of the nation's major denominations, and even those who have tried to resolve conflicts in committees in their local congregations, know differently. The struggles in American religion penetrate the denominational and congregational levels all too frequently.

We need to understand these conflicts within religious organizations. Yet it is often difficult to know exactly what is going on behind the scenes, or whether the conflicts one observes in one congregation are typical or atypical of the rifts in others. We can draw some inferences by viewing the large canvas of American religion at the national level. In some of what follows I have also tried to sharpen the focus by considering how the broader struggles in American religion have been manifest in one major Protestant denomination.

Of particular consequence today are three major points of tension within the relationship between American religion and American society: the state, the mass media, and higher education.

In all advanced industrial societies—and, indeed, in nearly all societies of all kinds—the role of the state has been expanding steadily in recent decades. We look to government to provide more and more services, to protect us against more and more of the uncertainties of life, and to enact the social and economic ideals we deem desirable. All this has come at a considerable price, as our tax bills remind us. Policymakers worry about how to stretch the public dollar as far as they can before resorting to unpopular increases in taxes. But social analysts worry about a potentially deeper problem—the "let George do it" attitude that comes with big government.

Increasingly, it seems, the more government does, the less capable we feel of making any difference in public life. Thus we are tempted to retreat into the quiet serenity of our private lives, tilling our own garden, so to speak, while the world goes by. Is this a valid concern, and if it is, how does it influence our commitments to our religious organizations?

In addition to the government, mass media play an ever increasing role in shaping our lives and our viewpoints. In the religious arena, the role played by mass media has focused increasingly on the nature and functioning of religious television programming. Whether we watch it or not—and millions do—religious television is having a dramatic impact on the ways we think of religion in American life, and it is certainly attempting to shape American life.

Much of the debate thus far has focused on the question of whether religious television, like the growth of big government, is encouraging people to spend more time at home in their living rooms by themselves, and thus is heightening the "privatization" of American religion. The question remains: do the electronic churches privatize our faith? Perhaps even more significantly, does faith undergo a qualitative change—both in public and in private—when it comes to us via television?

The place of higher education in American society has also been expanding dramatically in recent decades. This expansion has been a significant factor in the growing conflicts between religious liberals and religious conservatives. It has affected the balance between the two groups, and the two are often distinguished sharply in their overall levels of higher education.

Why should higher education have had such an impact on American religion in recent years? This question is not simply answered. For instance, it cannot be attributed only to different cognitive styles, such as an emphasis on reason rather than faith, or a naturalistic worldview as opposed to one that leaves room for the divine. To understand the relations between education and religion, we must probe more deeply into the institutional arrangements of both. We must understand the precariousness of knowledge in each realm—precariousness that leads to intellectual boundaries being set up that do not often reflect reason alone.

Much is changing in American religion. The mosaic of denominational pluralism that analysts described a generation ago no longer provides a useful image of the main contours of our faith. The tiles that made up that mosaic have been torn from their foundation. Some have been broken, and others have been scattered to form new patterns.

What those patterns are and why they have taken new shape are the questions we need to confront. Having answers to these questions is essential if we are to engage effectively in the vital debate over faith and values that is now being waged in our society.

Part I

CONTOURS OF THE FAITH

One   The Major Players

THE VIEW IS APPARENTLY WIDESPREAD that religion (at least some kinds of religion) should be more involved in public life. One may think of Jerry Falwell bringing the pulpit into politics or of Pat Robertson's presidential candidacy. For others, the civil rights activism of Martin Luther King, Jr., or the U.S. Catholic Bishops' statement on economic justice might come closer to symbolizing the kind of involvement desired. But the idea is much the same: that religious leaders and their followers should contribute actively to the definition of collective values.

This idea is hardly new. Falwell and King can be cited as advocates of greater public involvement on the part of religion but so can Martin Luther, John Calvin, Thomas Aquinas, and Saint Augustine. In our own history, religion has often played an important role in shaping the nature of public debate.

For social scientists, the idea of religion contributing to the collective good finds its greatest legitimacy, I suppose, in Alexis de Tocqueville. For as we know, more than 150 years ago, on his visit to the United States, Tocqueville expressed the belief that participation in voluntary associations, especially religious organizations, was a key to the strength and preservation of American democracy. In his view these associations provided the opportunity for people to come together, to discuss the critical issues affecting them collectively, to articulate public values, and to gain skills in public leadership. For the individual, the result was a sense of empowerment, a feeling of efficacy, an alleviation of normlessness and isolation. For the nation, the result was a strong set of natural, informal, grass-roots organizations that could undergird democracy. Tocqueville argued that as long as people were actively involved in voluntary associations, and as long as these associations were actively involved in the collective life of the nation, totalitarianism would be held at bay.[1]

A century and a half later, these ideas still seem particularly relevant. On the one hand, cultural analysts speak of widespread apathy toward the vital institutions that constitute our collective destiny. Narcissism is said to be rampant. Expressive individualism has turned large segments of the population in on themselves, causing them to be more interested in personal therapies than in public concerns. The proportion of the population that votes in national elections has steadily declined, and in many local elections this proportion is now as low as 5 percent of the eligible electorate. Polls show much cynicism toward government, business, and even organized religion. On the other hand, big government has grown bigger, despite the claims of many presidential hopefuls (and some incumbents) to be engaged in curtailing government and giving power back to the people. More and more of what affects us collectively seems to happen behind closed doors. Bureaucracy, rather than the town meeting, has become the symbol of government. Within the bureaucracies, self-styled patriotic entrepreneurs who seem to disdain the bright light of democratic processes decide on their own what the nation will and will not become involved in both domestically and in foreign affairs. More participation in voluntary associations, more involvement of religious organizations in discussing collective values, appears to be sorely needed.

It is, I believe, in this context that interest in the so-called third sector, independent sector, or nonprofit sector—the sector that includes the nation's churches and many of the charitable organizations they sponsor—has arisen. For it is in this sector that the kind of voluntary associations Tocqueville described still prevail. To be sure, there are other reasons as well for paying attention to this sector. For example, cutbacks in government expenditures for social welfare have

---

1. Alexis de Tocqueville, *Democracy in America,* 2 vols., tr. Henry Reeve, rev. Francis Bowen, ed. Phillips Bradley (New York: Vintage, repr. 1965) (originally published in 1835).

raised questions about the capacity of private nonprofit organizations to fill the gap. Social services such as care for the homeless, the jobless, and the hungry still depend heavily on the nonprofit sector. In this sector, too, many nonprofit organizations face uncertain futures: for example, church colleges face increasingly tough competition from tax-supported public institutions; church-related hospitals face similar competition from the new chains of for-profit health delivery systems; foundation officers struggle to make the most effective use of their endowments; and small community service organizations face constant pressures from inadequate donations of time and money. All these are serious and important questions, but the issues concerning the role of the voluntary sector as a whole in the public life of the nation—in shaping the discussion of public values and in preserving the democratic spirit—seem even more vital.

But having said this, what comes next? What do we need to know? What exactly is the voluntary sector? If it is one of the important players in shaping contemporary discussions about public values, who are the other players? What changes in the broader society do we need to understand? How does religion figure into the picture? What questions should guide our thinking?

THE THREE SECTORS OF AMERICAN SOCIETY

Before launching into any broader analysis of these issues, we need to be as clear as possible about what we mean by the voluntary sector in American society. I say "as clear as possible" because there is considerable ambiguity in the literature about how to conceptualize this sector. Some social theorists speak only of two major sectors in our society—the public and the private (i.e., government and the proprietary for-profit sector)—and consider voluntary associations simply as a subcategory of the public sector. For them, the churches are part of the public arena by definition—simply because they are not engaged in making profits. Others speak of three major players or sectors in American life, but disagree about the composition of each and the labels used to describe them. Nevertheless, we can put forth some tentative distinctions.

As a starting point, it is easiest to define the voluntary or "third" sector by saying what it is not. It is not the state, and it is not the marketplace. Or, put somewhat more specifically, the third sector consists of those activities and organizations that are not subsumed within the formal bureaucratic apparatus of government, on the one hand, and are not governed by the supply-demand-price mechanism or the profit incentives of the economic sector, on the other hand.

In the United States, the third sector (by this definition) is fairly closely associated with the so-called nonprofit sector. The nonprofit sector is demarcated both from the state and from the marketplace by legal distinctions. These legal distinctions prevent nonprofit organizations (for the most part) from engaging directly in political activities, on the one hand, and from earning and distributing profits, on the other hand. *Substantively,* therefore, the third sector includes the broad array of organizations and associations we usually place in the nonprofit sector: churches and parachurch organizations, fraternal associations, foundations, private charitable and welfare organizations, institutions of higher learning, civic and public affairs organizations, and many kinds of voluntary or not-for-profit health service agencies.

Defining the third sector in this way gives us a good first approximation of what it is we are discussing. Nevertheless, we immediately run into a thicket of troublesome questions—questions that have no simple answers but at least suggest some caveats to keep in mind. For instance, we may find it convenient to rely on tax codes and other legal distinctions to define the nonprofit sector. Yet we should not reify these distinctions. Other societies, with quite different legal codes, also have organizations that play functionally similar roles to the nonprofit sector in the United States. For example, the Soviet Union is said to have a stronger voluntary sector than most Westerners recognize, yet little of this sector is explicitly defined in Soviet legal codes. Or, to take another example, Japanese nonprofit associations function mainly as bureaus of the government, while the less formally organized and unofficially recognized community and neighborhood associations play a more important role in fulfilling the kinds of functions with which Tocqueville was concerned.

We also run into conceptual quicksand when we attempt to apply other standard ways of thinking to the third sector. For example, one way in which the social science literature has traditionally discussed this sector is in terms of dominant motivational styles. According to this literature, activities within the sphere of government are motivated by compulsion and fear because the *modus vivendi* of the state is coercion. In contrast, activities within the marketplace are motivated by utilitarian interests, even by selfish ego-oriented concerns. Thus, the third sector, as a sphere of "voluntary" activities, must be governed by altruistic motives.

We immediately run into difficulty in pursuing this line of analysis. For we know—even if we do not accept all of the classical economists' analysis—that market activities can themselves combine altruistic and utilitarian orientations. We know that government activity can also derive from altruistic inclinations (witness only the ideals that are still put forward in justification of so-called voluntary military service). We know just as well that activities within the nonprofit sector can contribute to ego gratifications such as status aspirations and self-esteem and can be engaged in for utilitarian reasons (such as publicity or establishing business contacts). Churches clearly cannot be set apart from the state or the marketplace only on the basis of what motives prevail.

If motivational analyses at the individual level prove difficult to sustain, so do discussions about the third sector's role in relation to so-called public or private realms of activity. For example, we would intuitively consider the kinds of discussions that go on in public universities as contributing as much to the third sector as we would the same kinds of discussions in private universities. We would probably be less inclined to include public elementary and secondary schools in the third sector. But we would be equally disinclined to include private corporations, whether their shares are considered "public" or not. Even within the nonprofit sector, we run into questions about how public or private some activities may be. For example, do we treat the local bowling league in the same way we treat the League of Women Voters? Or, in the religious sphere, is piety public or private? In relation to the third sector, is private prayer as relevant as public worship? What if it takes place in public schools? Is the local church supper as relevant as the National Council of Churches? Clearly, no simple relation exists between the third sector and distinctions between the public and private. We have to acknowledge that the voluntary sector is both public and private.

Where does that leave us? As a concept, the voluntary sector blends empirically with other concepts on all sides. Like all concepts in the social sciences, it is an *analytic* distinction—an abstraction from the complexities of social reality that we use to highlight certain problems and issues. It is a simplification, perhaps even an oversimplification.

In grasping for orienting models or metaphors, I have found myself drawn to a rather homely image, but one that seems to emphasize many of the important issues. This image likens society to an orange. The three main sectors of interest to us, then, can be likened to segments or wedges of the orange. On one side we have a fairly large segment called the state, on the other side another fairly large segment called the marketplace, and between the two a somewhat smaller wedge called the third sector or voluntary sector. All three have public aspects and private aspects. Indeed, we can imagine that the closer one moves to the periphery of the orange the more one is dealing with public issues; and the more one retreats into the center of the orange, the more one is involved with private activities.

This image works reasonably well if we also keep in mind that the boundaries among the three sectors of our society are neither distinct nor impermeable. The line between the state and the third sector is always a vague demarcation, as is the line between the third sector and the marketplace (and, for that matter, between the state and the marketplace). Our Constitution imposes a wall of separation between church and state, for instance, but we know that the state often passes laws that impinge on the churches, and religious leaders find ways of bringing their concerns to the attention of government officials. Our laws set up legal distinctions between for-profit corporations and the charitable associations that church groups sponsor; yet it sometimes becomes possible for these associations to spin off profit-making enterprises, and certainly corporate officials are not prevented from using their expertise to administer charitable organizations.

Moreover, resources of various kinds pass across the boundaries separating the three sectors. For example, the third sector may receive legitimacy from the state and in turn contribute ideas about collective goals that the state then takes responsibility for implementing. Church groups lobbying for higher or lower defense spending might be an example. From the marketplace the third sector receives, say, financial contributions and organizational models; in turn, the third sector gives social services that alleviate some of the social strains and dislocations produced by the marketplace.

Finally, if we compare different societies—or the same society at different periods—using this metaphor, we can see that the third sector may constitute a larger share of the whole in some instances and a smaller share in other instances. We can also imagine that the overall size of our metaphoric orange can vary—meaning that all three sectors can be bigger in some instances than in others.

THE FUNCTIONING OF THE VOLUNTARY SECTOR

Having in the back of our minds the kind of image I have been describing, we can now begin to place this image in a somewhat more theoretical framework that suggests particular questions worthy of examination. Actually, there are a number of such frameworks. For example, much of the research done on the third sector to date has implicitly conceived of this sector as a kind of pool requiring constant replenishing with the donations of time and money by individuals. Thus, questions have focused on the reasons why individuals give time and money to churches and other voluntary associations. At another level, the third sector has been thought of as a set of organizations that are somehow different from other organizations; therefore, questions have been asked about how these organizations come into being and what functions they fulfill. For example, some have argued that nonprofit organizations are especially suited to fulfilling functions that cannot be easily packaged, priced, and marketed, functions that appeal to too small a segment of the society to constitute an effective lobby or a profitable market, or functions that somehow require highly value-laden motivations or commitments.

These may all be worthwhile questions for consideration. Unfortunately, much of the discussion that has taken place in recent years concerning the voluntary sector appears to have strayed from the original philosophical concerns that generated interest in this sector. Indeed, one might say that discussions of the voluntary sector have increasingly been governed by values and norms derived from the other two sectors. Thus, from the business sector we have concerns about whether it is more efficient to run hospitals and clinics as nonprofit or for-profit enterprises; from government, questions about the effectiveness of administering social services through a single centralized hierarchy or a more decentralized, cooperative arrangement; and from both, questions about how particular nonprofit organizations can maximize their appeal to certain constituencies, how they can compete for scarce resources with other nonprofit organizations, how they can best be administered, and how they can manipulate legal constraints to their advantage. Such is the focus of the countless conferences and seminars held each year on the subject of philanthropy, and such is the focus of training to which fund-raisers and nonprofit organizations' staff are routinely exposed. The same concerns appear to be no less common among the bureaucrats and fund-raisers whose voices seem increasingly to predominate in religious circles. Yet, if we trace back-

ward through the philosophical literature, we discover a quite different set of concerns.

Perhaps the philosophical framework that is most readily available in the social science literature is a variant of the Tocquevillian argument that I have already mentioned—a variant that comes to us by
way of sociologists Emile Durkheim and more recently Robert Nisbet
and Peter Berger. Instead of the image of the third sector I presented
above, this tradition depicts a kind of hierarchical model. At the top stand
the central agents of the state, at the bottom lies the mass public (the
disaggregated individuals who constitute the membership of society and
who are organized only into nuclear family units), and in the middle we
find the voluntary associations that make up the third sector.

In this conception, the third sector functions mainly as a
mediating link between the mass citizenry and the state. For the citizenry, it provides "community," as Nisbet emphasizes, and "empowers
people," as Peter Berger says. For the state, it shields state functionaries
against the pressures of mass mobilization, articulates public interests,
and renders governing more convenient. In short, the third sector ultimately serves a political function, and that function is to articulate interests in such a way that totalitarianism is prevented and democracy
preserved.

This theoretical conception of the third sector is very much in
keeping with Tocqueville's concern about the role of voluntary associations in undergirding American democracy. It is, however, only part
of the story (and it could be shown, I believe, that this view also represents a serious misunderstanding of both Tocqueville and Durkheim). This conception is certainly more easily reconciled with the earlier Durkheimian views of society put forth in *The Division of Labor in
Society* than it is with Durkheim's mature views of social and cultural
integration which he presented in *The Elementary Forms of the Religious
Life*. In addition, although it seems to fit Tocqueville's view of American
democracy, it is not one that squares easily with Tocqueville's more
informed views of government in old-regime France or of government
under the revolution or Napoleon.

THE VOLUNTARY SECTOR AS A PUBLIC SPHERE

If we look more closely at this and other theoretical traditions from
which broad discussions of the third sector might derive, I believe we
arrive at a quite different picture. Rather than a hierarchical picture in

which the voluntary sector merely mediates the political interests of the mass citizenry to the state, we obtain a picture—more like the one I presented earlier—in which the third sector is related to the other two sectors but also functions somewhat autonomously. It functions—to anticipate what will hopefully become clearer momentarily—as a *public sphere*. That is, the third sector is of interest primarily as a locus of public discourse about the collective values of the society. It provides an arena in which fundamental values—both political and nonpolitical—can be discussed, experimented with, symbolized, and ritually enacted.

Reading Tocqueville within the historical context in which he wrote clearly gives us this impression of the voluntary sector as a public sphere. It was certainly not the France of the Terror, in which hundreds of Jacobin clubs mediated between the citizens of Paris and the government, that attracted Tocqueville. Nor was it the empire under Bonaparte, in which citizens' councils, departmental officials, and trade organizations created a highly corporatist version of society. Tocqueville was fundamentally more attracted to the old regime, and while he was critical of the excesses that resulted in its downfall, he also recognized the public debate it nurtured. For it was precisely in that context that the great contributions of Montesquieu, Voltaire, Diderot, and Rousseau were produced. When he turned to the United States, Tocqueville's interest in churches and other voluntary associations focused less on the tangible services they provided or even on their connections with agencies of the government. Rather, it was the fact that they were autonomous, that they involved a larger segment of the citizenry than in France, and that they contributed to the formation, as he put it, of public opinion.

Tocqueville's contemporary, Hegel, gives much the same impression, albeit in quite different terms. In *Philosophy of Right*, Hegel draws the familiar distinction between the state and civil society.[2] Writing against the backdrop of the Prussian state, Hegel was keenly aware of the state as formal bureaucracy. In comparison, civil society was less formally organized, more inclusive of the society, and much more diverse. It included not only the many civic, fraternal, and religious associations that characterized German society in the early nineteenth century but also trade associations and even business corporations. Indeed, civil society included almost everything except the bureaucratic state, on the one hand, and the private, familial life of the individual,

2. G. W. F. Hegel, *Philosophy of Right*, tr. T. M. Knox (Oxford: Oxford University Press, repr. 1952) (originally published in 1821).

on the other hand. Thus, civil society was clearly a public zone. But it was by no means subordinate to the state or merely concerned with political affairs. Rather, it was the seat from which sprang the collective ideals, the embodiment of moral virtue, with which Hegel was so concerned.

Of course, most of the credit for formulating the idea of the "public sphere" must be given to the German sociologist Jürgen Habermas. Because only his more recent formulations have appeared in English translation, Habermas has generally been understood as advancing a highly rationalistic, stark, even idealistic image of the public sphere—a kind of "communicative action" governed by enlightened, interest-free discussion of collective values. In his original study, *Strukturwandel der Offentlichkeit,* however, we gain a much richer sense of the public sphere.[3] It is diverse, divided into various subspheres or groupings constituted by interests and expertise. It exists in close interaction with the state but is clearly not the state nor subordinate to the state. Above all, it is oriented toward open discussion of basic societal goals. It is not governed by the technical or, as he puts it, "instrumental rationality" that dominates both government bureaucracy and the capitalist marketplace.

Habermas's model for the public sphere, like that of Tocqueville and Hegel, is the eighteenth century—the age of Enlightenment. It is there that we gain an initial sense of the conditions that may be essential for the existence of a public sphere. Here I am drawing on my own research rather than on Habermas's. In France, England, Scotland, and Prussia, where the debate about government and values more generally was most productive and innovative, we find the following: a substantial central bureaucracy that gave the society a sense of corporate identity and brought a sizable segment of the elite together in one place; an economy capable of sustaining a culture-producing elite; a number of autonomous salons, reading societies, debating clubs, philosophical associations, and centers of learning; and a relatively high degree of internal competition and conflict—conflict that not only motivated intensive examination of basic societal goals but also provided freedom for individuals to think creatively. That, I believe, is the specific historical context in which many of our democratic and liberal traditions were born, and it remains (often implicitly) the image of what we would like the third sector to contribute to our own society.

---

3. Originally published in 1962. For a translation, see Jürgen Habermas, *The Structural Transformation of the Public Sphere* (Cambridge: MIT Press, forthcoming).

The question, of course, is whether that model from the eighteenth century is still relevant and workable. And a vital question in the present context is what the role of religion may be within this model.

As to the first, we need to recognize above all that the third sector exists, as it were, at the mercy of the other two sectors. These sectors have changed dramatically since the eighteenth century—or even within the past half-century. The growth of the bureaucratic welfare state constitutes one of the significant factors affecting our understanding of the third sector as a public sphere. The changing character of the industrial or postindustrial economy constitutes the other significant factor.

By all indications, the bureaucratic welfare state has expanded in scope and significance to unprecedented proportions in the twentieth century and especially in the years since World War II. Government expenditures as a percent of the Gross National Product have risen by 50 percent, taxes in constant dollars have tripled, and federal court cases have quadrupled. More generally, the state is organized into larger bureaucratic agencies, employs a larger percentage of the population, supplies more services, and regulates more aspects of personal and social life than ever before.

As for the economy, bureaucratization has also kept pace in this sector. Regional and national markets have now become more fully integrated, thereby intensifying levels of competition, and a majority of U.S. products now compete for sales in international markets. Standardization and technical efficiency have become more important as economic criteria. Technology itself increasingly defines the limits of conceivable social and economic goals. The so-called service sector now contributes more to the Gross National Product than the manufacturing and agricultural sectors combined. Within this sector especially, professionalization and higher levels of technical competence are requisite job expectations.

These developments clearly have important implications for assessing the present and future roles of the nonprofit, voluntary sector in general, and for understanding the social location of the churches. For example, as government bureaucracy expands, the potential for more and more of the society's policies being determined behind closed doors rather than through open public discussion becomes a frightening reality. This same expansion, to the extent that it involves an effective provision of social services under government auspices, also strips voluntary organizations of their raison d'être. Having fewer opportunities to contribute tangibly to the public good, these organizations may well lose their claim to participation in the determination of collective values as well.

The expansion of industrial and postindustrial capitalism also carries significant implications. In forcing private firms into a closer alliance with government, as many analysts have suggested, this expansion potentially reduces some of the crosscutting social conflict that has traditionally provided a space for the third sector to engage in critical public discourse. As the for-profit sector has expanded into the provision of social services—hospitals being the most vivid example—it has not only reduced the incentive for voluntary associations to continue supplying these services, but has also on occasion consciously brought governmental pressure to bear on the voluntary sector to eliminate its legal protections. And as the service economy has become more professionalized, only the professional elite has the cultural capital with which to engage in effective discourse about public issues.

There is, in short, a very real danger of the bureaucratic welfare state and the advanced institutions of planned corporate capitalism simply squeezing out the third sector, thereby robbing the society of a traditionally significant forum for public discourse about collective values. Whether this danger is present and real is, of course, more difficult to determine. For example, some would argue that effective discussion of societal goals can still take place, even if it is limited to government agencies and corporate boardrooms, perhaps with less overt conflict and with greater efficiency. Others suggest that the changes in recent years in the state and in the marketplace are unlikely to squeeze out the third sector, but these changes may radically alter the composition of the third sector.

Government-sponsored nonprofit agencies may prevail, while those lacking government support will falter. According to this prediction, more and more of the voluntary sector will be made up of specialized social service agencies, while less and less will derive from the churches because churches, among all voluntary associations, are most restricted from acquiring government resources. In addition, those associations that can adapt to the demands of bureaucratic organization and technical competence will fare better than those that cling to old-fashioned modes of operation. If the composition of the third sector is altered, then surely the mix of public values that are expressed will be transformed as well—which brings us to the question of religion's role in the third sector.

AMERICAN RELIGION IN THE PUBLIC SPHERE

There is little indication in recent decades that American religion has undergone what might be termed "secularization" in any absolute sense. According to most of the standard measures, such as participation in organized religion, belief in God, and belief in an afterlife, religious commitment is as strong now as it was thirty-five or forty years ago.

But American religion has not been unaffected by the social changes I have just mentioned. Its institutional base is deeply embedded in the broader social environment, and its orientation is toward active engagement with the secular world. Thus, sometimes inadvertently and often by conscious design, American religion has adapted to a changing social situation, and this adaptation has significant implications for understanding the role of religion in the third sector.

One of the most important, albeit gradual, changes that has taken place in American religion since World War II has been a decline in the tensions between Protestants and Catholics, between Christians and Jews, and between different Protestant denominations. In the immediate postwar years, these tensions gave American religion its internal structure and influenced many of the activities of the major religious bodies. By the end of the 1960s, however, and even to a greater extent by the end of the 1970s, the effects of the ecumenical movement, of the more general attitudes of toleration being promoted by higher education, and of regional migration, intermarriage, and other forms of social mixing were having notable effects. Traditional organizational lines were still there, but these lines meant far less than they had only a few decades before. People switched denominations with alacrity, married across faith boundaries with increasing ease, and generally saw little reason to revere the distinctive traditions of their own faith—or at least to let these loyalties interfere with social interaction.

At the same time that these traditional distinctions were declining in importance, a host of new, more specialized religious interest groups were being founded. Women's caucuses and black caucuses, parachurch groups for the young and the old, missions and evangelism organizations, and occupationally based associations (such as Christian Cowboys and Pilots for Jesus) came on the scene in increasing numbers. Many of these special purpose groups were at least indirectly responsive to changes in the government and in the economy. For example, many represented religious responses to government initiatives in the areas of civil rights, social services, and entitlement programs. Others responded to the growth of higher education and the increasing professionalization of the work force.

In their activities, they performed the functions that Tocqueville would have expected voluntary associations to perform. They gathered together groups of like-minded individuals, reinforced their particular interests, symbolized these interests and values to the rest of the nation, and contributed to the formation of public discourse. Yet, coupled with other changes, they also contributed to the growing polarization of religion's response to the public sphere.

This polarization developed gradually. It came about partly in response to the civil rights movement and the Vietnam War. As we know, in these years significant shares of the clergy and a minority of the laity began to rethink the ways in which religious convictions should interact with the collective conscience. Observing a marked hiatus between professed values and actual behavior in the areas of race relations and foreign policy, many religious leaders began to advocate less talk and more direct action. In addition, rising levels of education contributed to an increasing gap in religious orientations between the better educated and the less well educated. The better educated typically adopted more liberal and relativistic belief patterns and favored active engagement in social issues; the less well educated followed more traditional lines in belief and practice and came increasingly to focus on issues of personal morality. Gradually, beginning in the late 1940s and extending through the 1970s, the evangelical movement (as it called itself) also forged strong national organizations, grew in numbers, and by the 1980s had become, in its own right, a major voice in the public arena.

A high degree of pluralism also still prevails in American religion. This pluralism contributes significantly to the vitality of the public sphere in general and of the third sector in particular. A healthy system of cultural checks and balances exists among the major faiths in the United States. Whenever a distinctly Presbyterian view is expressed, it is sure to be countered—or at least modified—by a Lutheran view, a Catholic view, and a Jewish view, not to mention dozens of other possibilities. The effects of pluralism are often especially evident in the formation of special interest groups concerned with articulating certain values in the public sphere. Let an abortion rights group or a gay caucus start in one branch of American religion, and soon dozens of complementary and competing groups will be founded in other segments of the religious community. The very proliferation of these groups ensures that a larger total share of the religious community will have some means of voicing its views, and the ensuing competition among them ensures that a great deal of energy will be expended in formulating, explaining, and elaborating positions on collective values.

Thus far in our nation's history, religious organizations have done a remarkable job of adapting to new opportunities and issues. The use of religious television is an example of religious groups exploiting new technologies for influencing the public agenda. The debates that have arisen over abortion, nuclear disarmament, sanctuary, and economic justice attest to the continuing ability of religious organizations to engage in discussions of the major issues of the day.

Nevertheless, some of the ways in which religion has traditionally participated in the third sector have been undermined by the political and economic developments we have just considered. For example, prior to World War II, religion provided much of the nation's higher education, sponsored many of the nation's leading hospitals, and carried the lion's share of services for the elderly, handicapped, and homeless. Today, most people look to government to fulfill these functions.

Perhaps an even more serious development, though, is the polarization that has come to characterize American religion—the deep cultural divide between conservative or evangelical Christians, on one side, and religious liberals and secular humanists, on the other side. According to public opinion polls, this cleavage is fraught with considerable misgiving and stereotyping on both sides. It divides the nation into two opposing camps that are approximately equal in numbers, and it cuts directly through most of the nation's major denominational families and faith traditions.

We shall examine this polarity and the sources behind it in the next chapter. Let it suffice here to say that, to a significant degree, this polarity is itself a function of religion's involvement in the public life of the nation. It has been reinforced by a fundamental ambivalence—what Marxists would call a "contradiction"—in the relation between the other two sectors.

One side of this contradiction expresses the traditional laissez faire view of government, a view that charges government with the protection of free market activities, that favors minimalist government intervention in redistributional policies, and that asserts the importance of government in protecting domestic security and upholding the essential moral fiber of the nation. The other side champions the more interventionist role of government as a regulator and promoter of the economy and especially as a corrective agency to overcome whatever injustices and inequalities may be produced by the untrammeled operation of market principles. Neither of these views has been consistently associated with one religious faction or the other. But both religious conservatives and religious liberals have found periodic support for their views from public officials who have advocated one or the other of these positions.

As religious liberals and religious conservatives have engaged in public debate, the public role of religion has seemingly increased. Yet one can ask whether this polarization has been entirely beneficial for the expression of public values. Increasingly, it appears, both sides take their cues from each other and allow political considerations to dictate their choice of means and ends. Genuine alternatives often seem to be drowned out by these strident voices.

I have tried to suggest, then, that religion's role in the third sector—in the public sphere—is neither guaranteed nor inherently productive of harmonious exchange. Serious transformations are taking place in the state and in the marketplace that threaten to undermine the third sector, to replace it with some other forum for public discourse, or at least to modify its composition. Within this vortex, the public role of religion still seems strong, if not undiminished. But the engagement of American religion in public discourse generates conflict within the religious community—conflict that may be damaging to the very values that the religious community wishes to uphold. Many of these issues are normative, themselves requiring consideration from practical and prescriptive points of view. Many are also empirical, demanding additional examination before any normative pronouncements are made.

Two

Old Fissures, New Fractures

IN THE OPENING LINES of his hauntingly memorable description of the Battle of Waterloo, Victor Hugo makes a startling observation: "If it had not rained on the night of June 17, 1815, the future of Europe would have been different. A few drops more or less tipped the balance against Napoleon. For Waterloo to be the end of Austerlitz, Providence needed only a little rain, and an unseasonable cloud crossing the sky was enough for the collapse of a world."[1] What is startling is not the idea that the future of Europe, or even the outcome of the battle, hinged on something as seemingly trivial as an unexpected rainstorm.

Such explanations fill the annals of military history. Had not the British expeditionary force been able to evacuate from Dunkirk under cover of heavy fog during the week of May 26, 1940, the German army might well have gone on to win the war. Those who tread the battlefields near Gettysburg, Pennsylvania, view the heights along Culp's Hill and Cemetery Ridge, and wonder what the outcome would have been had Lee's troops occupied those favored positions instead of Meade's. The great turning points of history sometimes appear to hinge less on what people do than the conditions under which they have to do it. The flukes of nature—or the hand of God—intervene willfully at fortuitous moments.

1. Victor Hugo, Les Misérables (New York: New American Library, 1987), p. 309.

19

Yet we in contemporary society, schooled as we have been in the complexities of history, know how tenuous these arguments often prove to be. Battles may be won or lost on the basis of a sudden turn of weather, but wars are not and neither is the course of history.

What if, by some chance, Lee's troops had occupied the heights at Gettysburg? Would Meade's then have run the bloody gauntlet that became immortalized as "Pickett's charge"? Or would the Federal army have faded away to fight on more opportune terms? We learn from modern analysts of the battle that Lee was forced to fight, despite the unfavorable terrain, because he desperately needed to win. Supplies were running low and Confederate agents needed to be able to demonstrate to their European creditors that they could win. The reason supplies were running low lay deep in the South's agrarian economy (cf. the North's industrial economy) and even deeper in the triangular trade that had developed between the South, Great Britain, and West Africa. Lee was forced to fight; Meade could have slipped away.

As we proceed with Victor Hugo's account, what actually startles us is that he succeeds so well in defending his thesis. A soggy battlefield was indeed a decisive factor. But as so often is the case in Hugo's narratives, it was the larger terrain—and the uncertainties inherent in this terrain—that constituted the framework in which the decisions of the two commanders had to be made. An unexpected rainstorm made it impossible for Napoleon to deploy the full force of his artillery. He could not have anticipated this factor, an element of the battle that in essence remained obscure.

The *quid obscurum* in Hugo's account, though, is at once more simple and straightforward than this and more elusive. Running through the battlefield, interposed directly between the two armies, was a ditch. It extended across the entire line that Napoleon's cavalry would have to charge. It was a deep chasm, made by human hands, the result of a road that had been cut like a knife through the natural terrain. It was hidden from view. The cavalry charged, and then faced the terror. Hugo recounts:

> There was the ravine, unexpected, gaping right at the horses' feet, twelve feet deep between its banks. The second rank pushed in the first, the third pushed in the second; the horses reared, lurched backward, fell onto their rumps, and struggled writhing with their feet in the air, piling up and throwing their riders; no means to retreat; the whole column was nothing but a projectile. The momentum to crush the English crushed the French. The inexorable ravine could not yield until it was

filled; riders and horses rolled in together helter-skelter, grinding against each other, making common flesh in this dreadful gulf, and when this grave was full of living men, the rest marched over them and went on. Almost a third of Dubois's brigade sank into the abyss.[2]

The *quid obscurum* was quite literally a hidden fracture with enormous consequences.

The second, and deeper, meaning of Hugo's reference to the *quid obscurum* is that of the broader uncertainties evoked by the clash of two armies. Only in the heat of battle do the unforeseen contingencies become evident; only then do the plans of the commanding generals prove to have missed important features of the broader terrain. In the struggling line of soldiers engaged in hand-to-hand combat one begins to realize that the expenditures are greater than expected. The consequences of seemingly unimportant conditions turn out to be incalculable. It is left to the historian to calculate, with the advantage of hindsight, the role of these previously obscured realities.

THE GREAT FRACTURE IN AMERICAN RELIGION

My purpose in drawing attention to Hugo's discussion is also twofold. At the more literal level, like the ravine cutting across the plateau of Mont-Saint-Jean, a great fracture runs through the cultural terrain on which the battles of religion and politics are now being fought. It is a fracture that deserves our attention. For it is of recent creation, a human construction, unlike the timeless swells of culture through which it has been cut. It has become a mire of bitter contention, consuming the energies of religious communities and grinding their ideals into the grime of unforeseen animosities. At a broader level, this fracture also symbolizes the unplanned developments in the larger terrain that did not become evident until the battles themselves began to erupt. With the advantage of hindsight, we can now discover the importance of these developments. We can see how the present controversies in American religion were affected by broader changes in the society— the consequences of which remained obscure at the time but have now become painfully transparent.

The ravine running through the culturescape of American religion is as real as the one made by the road between the two vil-

2. Ibid., pp. 328-29.

lages on the Belgian border, though it differs from that Belgian ravine
in one important respect. It is not simply a fissure in the physical environment, a ditch that creates the downfall of one of the protagonists.
It is to a much greater extent the product of the battle itself. The chasm
dividing American religion into separate communities has emerged
largely from the struggle between these two communities. It may have
occurred, as I shall suggest shortly, along a fault line already present
in the cultural terrain. But it has been dug deeper and wider by the
skirmishes that have been launched across it.

Depending on whose lens we use to view it, we can describe
this fissure in any number of ways. Television evangelist Jimmy Swaggart has described it as a gulf between those who believe in the Judeo-
Christian principles on which our country was founded and those who
believe in the "vain philosophies of men." On one side are the "old-
fashioned" believers in "the word of Almighty God" who are often
maligned as "poor simpletons"; on the other side are the "so-called
intelligentsia," those who believe they are great because they "are more
intelligent than anyone else," "socialists," believers in "syphilitic
Lenin," and the burdened masses who have nothing better to get ex-
cited about than football and baseball games.[3] In contrast, a writer for
the *New York Times* depicted it as a battle between "churches and
church-allied groups" who favor freedom, democracy, and the rights
of minorities, on the one hand, and a right-wing fringe interested in
setting up a theocracy governed by a "dictatorship of religious values,"
on the other hand.[4]

Apart from the colors in which the two sides are portrayed,
though, one finds general agreement on the following points: (a) the
reality of the division between two opposing camps; (b) the predominance of "fundamentalists," "evangelicals," and "religious conservatives" in one and the predominance of "religious liberals," "humanists,"
and "secularists" in the other; and (c) the presence of deep hostility
and misgiving between the two.

An official of the National Council of Churches summarized
the two positions, and the views of each toward the other, this way:
"Liberals abhor the smugness, the self-righteousness, the absolute cer-
tainty, the judgmentalism, the lovelessness of a narrow, dogmatic faith.

3. From a broadcast in February 1987 titled "What is the Foundation for Our
Philosophy of Christianity?" I wish to thank Victoria Chapman for the transcription of
this sermon.
4. E. J. Dionne, Jr., "Religion and Politics," *New York Times,* 15 September 1987.

[Conservatives] scorn the fuzziness, the marshmallow convictions, the inclusiveness that makes membership meaningless—the 'anything goes' attitude that views even Scripture as relative. Both often caricature the worst in one another and fail to perceive the best."[5]

To suggest that American religion is divided neatly into two communities with sharply differentiated views is, of course, to ride roughshod over the countless landmarks, signposts, hills, and gullies that actually constitute the religious landscape. Not only do fundamentalists distinguish themselves from evangelicals, but each brand of religious conservatism is divided into dozens of denominational product lines. Similar distinctions can be made on the religious left. In the popular mind, though, there does seem to be some reality to the cruder, binary way of thinking.

A national survey, conducted several years ago (even before some of the more acrimonious debates over the role of religion in politics had arisen), found both a high level of awareness of the basic division between religious liberals and conservatives and a great deal of genuine hostility between the two. When asked to classify themselves, 43 percent of those surveyed identified themselves as religious liberals and 41 percent said they were religious conservatives. The public is thus divided almost equally between the two categories, and only one person in six was unable or unwilling to use these labels.[6]

The ways in which self-styled liberals and conservatives answered other questions also seem to lend some validity to the two categories. As one would expect, conservatives were much more likely than liberals to identify themselves as evangelicals, to believe in a literal interpretation of the Bible, to say they had had a "born-again" conversion experience, to indicate that they had tried to convert others to their faith, and to hold conservative views on issues such as abortion and prayer in public schools. Liberals were less likely than conservatives to attend church or synagogue regularly, but a majority af-

---

5. Peggy L. Shriver, "The Paradox of Inclusiveness-that-Divides," *Christian Century* (January 21, 1984): 194.

6. At the extremes, the public was also about equally divided: 19 percent said they were very liberal; 18 percent, very conservative. These figures are from a survey conducted in June 1984 by the Gallup Organization under a grant from the Robert Schuller Ministries. Some of the study's findings were reported in the May and June, 1986, issues of *Emerging Trends*, a publication edited by George Gallup, Jr. The results of additional analyses of these data appear in Robert Wuthnow, *The Restructuring of American Religion: Society and Faith since World War II* (Princeton: Princeton University Press, 1988).

firmed the importance of religion in their lives, tended to regard the Bible as divinely inspired (but not to be taken literally), and held liberal views on a variety of political and moral issues.

Some denominations tended to consist of more conservatives than liberals, or vice versa. But generally, the major denominational families and faith traditions—Methodists, Lutherans, Presbyterians, Baptists, Catholics, Jews—were all divided about equally between religious conservatives and religious liberals. In other words, the cleavage between conservatives and liberals tends not, for the most part, to fall along denominational lines. It is a cleavage that divides people within the same denominations—as recent struggles within the Southern Baptist Convention, the Episcopal Church, the Presbyterian Church, U.S.A., and the Roman Catholic Church all attest.

The study also demonstrated the extent to which the relations between religious liberals and religious conservatives have become rife with conflict. A majority of the public surveyed said the conflict between religious liberals and conservatives is an area of "serious tension." A substantial majority of both groups said they had had unpleasant, or at best "mixed," relations with the other group. These relations were said to have taken place in fairly intimate settings: in one's church, among friends and relatives, even within the same Bible study or fellowship groups. Moreover, each side held a number of negative images of the other. Liberals saw conservatives as rigid, intolerant, and fanatical. Conservatives described liberals as shallow, morally loose, unloving, and unsaved.

The study also demonstrated that, unlike other kinds of prejudice and hostility, the ill feelings separating religious liberals and religious conservatives *did not mitigate* as the two groups came into greater contact with one another. The more each side came into contact with the other, and the more knowledge it gained about the other, the less it liked the other.

Viewed normatively, such levels of animosity and tension between religious liberals and conservatives are disturbing. We might expect nothing better from communists and capitalists or Democrats and Republicans. But deep within the Hebrew and Christian traditions lies an ethic of love and forgiveness. In congregation after congregation prayers are routinely offered for unity among the faithful. Creeds are recited stating belief in the one, holy, catholic church. And homilies are delivered on Jesus' injunction to love one's neighbor as oneself.

If these findings are disturbing, they are not, however, surprising. They accord with the way in which American religion is portrayed in the media and in pulpits, and with the way in which American religion seems to function. The major newspapers and television networks routinely publicize the bizarre activities of fundamentalists and evangelicals: the conservative governor who prays with his pastor and hears God tell him to run for the presidency, the television preacher who prays (successfully, it turns out) that an impending hurricane will be averted from the Virginia coast, the fundamentalists in Indiana who deny their children proper schooling and medical care, the evangelical counselor in California who is sued by the family of a patient who committed suicide, the deranged member of a fundamentalist church in Maine who shoots down his fellow parishioners with a shotgun.

Conservative television preachers and conservative religious publications make equally vitriolic comments about their liberal foes: how an Episcopal bishop is condoning sexual permissiveness within his diocese, how Methodist liberals are encouraging homosexuality among the denomination's pastors, how zealous clergy in the nuclear disarmament movement are selling the country out to the Russians, how religious conservatives are being discriminated against in colleges and universities. It is little wonder that the labels begin to stick. Sooner or later it does in fact begin to appear as if the world of faith is divided between two belligerent superpowers.

But this picture of the religious world is not simply a creation of the sensationalist media. At the grass roots, one can readily find denunciations of liberalism from conservative pulpits and diatribes against fundamentalism from liberal pulpits. One can readily observe the split between liberals and conservatives in church meetings and discussion groups. Liberals freely express doubts about the historical authenticity of the Bible. Conservatives appeal for greater faith in the supernatural, the miraculous, and argue for more emphasis on sin and personal salvation. Beneath the innocent statements of each are deeper feelings about right and wrong, truth and error.

Beyond these simple exchanges, the two also isolate themselves in different communities of support and action: liberals in the nurturing environment of the local peace concerns fellowship, the forum on AIDS, the movement to lobby for equitable and affordable housing; conservatives in the womb of Bible study groups and prayer fellowships.

One can also readily observe the polarizing tendencies of national issues on the religious environment. Pick up the latest issue of *Christian Century* or *Christianity Today*; observe the number of articles that deal with politics and note the paucity of material on theology or

even personal spirituality. Or open the mail and count the letters from
Moral Majority, Christian Voice, People for the American Way, the
American Civil Liberties Union. The issues are now national rather
than local or regional. They concern an appointment to the Supreme
Court, a constitutional amendment on abortion, a preacher running
for president. They are supported by one faction of the religious community and opposed by another. They induce polarization.

But to say that the chasm between religious liberals and conservatives exists for many reasons is still only to describe it—to parade
the colors of the troops engaged in the great battle of which this conflict consists. It is a chasm deepened and widened by political debate.
It is a chasm around which religious communities' participation in
public affairs divides. It has become a predictable feature of the contemporary debate over church-state relations. To understand it, though,
we must look at broader developments in the social terrain. We must
try to discover why this particular fracture line existed in the cultural
geography in the first place.

A CLOSER LOOK AT THE CULTURAL GEOGRAPHY

In one sense, of course, the fracture line can be found in the soil of
American religion as far back as the years immediately after the Civil
War. Even in the eighteenth century and during the first half of the
nineteenth century one can identify the beginnings of a division between religious conservatives and religious liberals insofar as one considers the effects of the Enlightenment on elite culture. Skepticism,
atheism, anticlericalism, and of course deism constitute identifiable alternatives to the popular piety of Methodists and Baptists and to the
conservative orthodoxy of Roman Catholics, Jews, Presbyterians, and
others during this period. But to an important degree the potential
division between conservatism and liberalism before the Civil War is
overshadowed by the deeper tensions to which the society is subject.
Nationalism and regionalism, differences between the culture of the
Eastern seaboard and the expanding Western territories, and increasingly the tensions between North and South provide the major
divisions affecting the organization of American religion.

Not until the termination of these hostilities and the resump-
tion of material progress after the Civil War does it become possible
for the gap between religious conservatives and liberals to gain importance. Gradually in these years the discoveries of science, the new ideas

of Charles Darwin, and by the end of the century the beginnings of a
national system of higher education provide the groundwork for a
liberal challenge to religious conservatism. Of course, the culmination
of these changes comes at the turn of the century in the modernist
movement and its increasingly vocal opponent, the fundamentalists.

In the long view, the present division between religious
liberals and religious conservatives can be pictured simply as a continuation or outgrowth of this earlier conflict. The inevitable forces of
modernization produced a secular tendency in American religion, a
tendency that condoned greater individual freedom in matters of the
spirit and voiced skepticism toward a faith based in divine revelation,
and this tendency evoked a reactionary movement in which religious
conservatism was preserved.

That, as I say, is the impression gained from taking a long view
of American history. If one takes a more limited perspective, though,
a rather different impression emerges. One is able to focus more directly on the immediate contours of the religious environment and to see
how these contours are in the short term shaped by specific events. I
suppose that this is the advantage of taking the perspective of the
sociologist—which seldom extends much before World War II.

At the close of that war, the condition of American religion
was quite different than it is now. It contained seeds that were to ger-
minate and grow, like weeds in the concrete, widening the cracks that
have now become so visible. But the basic divisions ran along other
lines. Tensions between Protestants and Catholics had reached new
heights as immigration and natural increase contributed to the growth
of the Catholic population. Tensions between Christians and Jews also
ran deep, even though they were often less visible than the conflicts
dividing Protestants and Catholics. There was, as Will Herberg described it a few years later, a "tripartite division" in American religion:
to be American was to be Protestant, Catholic, or Jewish.[7]

In addition, denominational boundaries also played an important role in giving structure to the Protestant branch of this tripartite
arrangement. Ecumenical services were beginning to erode some of
these boundaries (often for the explicit purpose of displaying Protestant unity against the threat of papal expansion). But ethnic, national,
and geographic divisions—as well as theological and liturgical divisions—continued to reinforce denominational separatism.

7. Will Herberg, *Protestant-Catholic-Jew* (Garden City, NY: Doubleday-Anchor,
1955).

In all of this, there was little evidence of any basic split between liberals and conservatives. To be sure, fundamentalism was alive and well. But its very success proved in a deeper sense to be its limitation. By the mid-1930s, fundamentalist spokesmen had largely conceded their defeat in the major Protestant denominations and had withdrawn to form their own organizations. As the Great Depression, and then the rationing imposed by the war, made travel more difficult, these organizations also grew farther apart from one another. By the end of the war, they consisted mainly of small, isolated splinter groups on the fringes of the mainline denominations.

Most of the population that continued to believe in such doctrinal tenets as biblical inerrancy, the divinity of Jesus, and the necessity of personal salvation remained within these larger denominations. Even the official policies of these denominations reflected what would now be considered a strong conservative emphasis. Evangelism, door-to-door canvassing of communities, revival meetings, biblical preaching, missions—all received prominent support.

Also of significance was the fact that many of the more outspoken conservative religious leaders were unobtrusively beginning to build their own organizations. At this point, however, these leaders were able to build quietly and were content largely to maintain ties with the major denominations, rather than break away like their fundamentalist counterparts.

There were certainly differences of opinion among believers about such matters as the literal inspiration of the Bible or the role of churches in political affairs. But these were as yet not the subject of mass movements or of widely recognized cultural divisions. Only the terms "fundamentalist" and "liberal" suggest continuity between this period and our own; a more careful examination of issues, personalities, and organizations indicates discontinuity.

FISSURE LINES IN THE RELIGIOUS LANDSCAPE

In the years immediately following World War II we do find evidence of the conditions that were to predispose American religion to undergo a major transformation in the decades that followed. Three such predisposing conditions stand out.

First, American religion was on the whole extraordinarily strong. The largest churches now counted members in the thousands. Overall, the number of local churches and synagogues ranged in the hundreds of thousands. Some denominations sported budgets in the tens of millions. Collectively, religious organizations took in approximately $800 million annually—as historian Harold Laski observed, this figure exceeded the budget of the entire British government.[8]

In comparison with Europe, the American churches were especially strong. They had not been subjected to the same limitations on government spending that the churches in England, France, and Germany had faced, nor had they encountered the mass withdrawal of the working classes that these churches had experienced; and of course they had not been subject to the extensive destruction resulting from the war. They had been weakened by the Depression and by shortages of building materials during the war. But curiously, perhaps, this very weakness turned out to be a strength as well. It prompted major building programs after the war, allowed the churches to relocate in growing neighborhoods, and generally encouraged what was to become known as the religious revival of the 1950s.

The critical feature of the churches' massive institutional strength for the coming decades was religion's ability to adjust to a changing environment. Rather than simply wither away—or maintain itself in quiet contemplative seclusion—it adapted to the major social developments of the postwar period. In this sense, we owe much of the present controversy in American religion to the simple fact that it had remained a strong institutional force right up to the second half of the twentieth century.

The second predisposing condition was the strong "this-worldly" orientation of American religion. Not only was it able to adapt to changing circumstances; it also engaged itself actively in the social environment by its own initiative. When the war ended, religious leaders looked to the future with great expectancy. They recognized the opportunities that lay ahead. They were also mindful of the recurrent dangers they faced.

Indeed, a prominent theme in their motivational appeals focused on the combination of promise and peril. For instance, a resolution passed by the Federal Council of Churches in 1945 declared: "We are living in a uniquely dangerous and promising time."[9] It was a dangerous time because of the recurrent likelihood of war, the widely anticipated return to a depressed economy after the war-induced

8. Harold Laski, *The American Democracy* (New York: Viking, 1948), p. 283.
9. "The Churches and World Order," reprinted in *Christian Century* (February 7, 1945): 174-77.

boom had ended, and of course the invention of nuclear weapons. It was a promising time because of new opportunities for missionary work and evangelism.

The stakes were high, so persistent activism was the desired response. In the words of a Methodist minister, who reminded his audience of the perilous opportunities facing them: "That requires . . . a great godly company of men and women with no axe to grind, desiring only to save, serve, help and heal."[10] The result was that religious organizations deliberately exposed their flanks to the influences of their environment. Programs were initiated, education was encouraged, preaching confronted issues of the day—all of which, like the rain on Napoleon's troops, would reveal the churches' dependence on the conditions of their terrain.

The third predisposing factor was reflected in the relation understood to prevail between religion and the public sphere. This factor is especially important to understand, because it provides a vivid contrast with the ways in which we now conceive of religion's influence in the political arena. In the 1940s and 1950s there appears to have been a fairly widespread view among religious leaders, theologians, and even social scientists that values and behavior were closely related. Find out what a person's basic values were, and you could pretty well predict that person's behavior. If persons valued democracy, they could be counted on to uphold it in their behavior. If a person worked hard and struggled to get ahead, you could be pretty sure that person valued success and achievement.

More broadly, writers also extended this connection to society. A nation's culture consisted essentially of values, and these values were arranged in a hierarchy of priority. The society was held together by this hierarchy of values. It generated consensus and caused people to behave in similar ways.

For religious leaders, this way of conceiving things was very convenient. It meant that the way to shape people's lives was by shaping their values, and this was what the churches did best: they preached and they taught. They influenced the individual's system of values. They shaped the individual's conscience.

The churches' conduit to the public arena was thus through the individual's conscience. Shape a churchperson's values, and you could rest assured that your influence would be carried into the public sphere.

10. C. Stanley Lowell, "The Conversion of America," *Christian Century* (September 29, 1949): 1134.

That person would vote according to his or her conscience, would manifest high values in his or her work, would behave charitably, ethically, honestly. All the churches needed to do was preach and teach.

This view also gained support from the public arena itself. Public officials spoke frequently and fervently about their commitment to high moral principles. They lauded the work of religious leaders in reinforcing these principles. Truman, Eisenhower, Dulles, and others spoke of their own religious faith and commended this faith as a source of societal cohesion and strength. It was easy for religious leaders to believe that their efforts were really having an impact.

Already, though, there were signs that this worldview was coming apart. The problem was not that political leaders were suspected of hypocrisy, although this may have been the case. Nor was the problem, as some have suggested, that this was basically a Protestant view, and thus was being undermined by the growing pluralism of the society. Catholic and Jewish leaders in the 1950s articulated it too. The idea was not that religious faith channeled behavior in specifically Protestant or Catholic or Jewish directions. The idea—at least the one expressed in public contexts—was that a deep religious faith gave the individual moral strength, conviction, the will to do what was right.

But the premises on which this worldview itself was based were beginning to be questioned. Doubts were beginning to be expressed about the basic connection between values and behavior. What if one's basic values did not translate into actual behavior? What if one's behavior did not stem from one's convictions but was influenced by other factors?

At this time, these questions were only raised occasionally. But the very fact that they could be raised suggested the presence of a cultural fissure, a fault line along which a more serious fracture could open up. Values constituted one category, behavior another. The two categories were connected—had to be connected closely for arguments about the impact of conscience on public affairs to be credible. But this connection itself was becoming tenuous.

YEARS OF STRUGGLE

How then did these predisposing conditions in the 1950s become transformed to produce the chasm between religious liberals and conservatives that we experience at the present? How did Herberg's tripartite system, in which the basic religious and *religio-political* divisions occurred between Protestants and Catholics and between Christians and Jews, come to be replaced by what some have called a "two-party system"?

The answer is complex, of course, because it involves not only the relations among all the major religious groupings but also the relations between religion and the forces shaping the broader society. It is, however, enormously important, for it brings together all the decisive factors that have shaped American religion in the period since World War II. We can touch on only the basic contours here.

In picturing the transformation as a tripartite division being replaced by a two-party system, we should not think that the latter simply superimposed itself on the former or that the one led directly into the other. It is helpful to divide the process in two and seek answers for each of its phases separately. The first phase (not chronologically but analytically) amounted to an erosion of the basic divisions constituting the tripartite system. The second phase amounted to developments reinforcing a new, different cleavage between liberals and conservatives. These processes combined to create what many have sensed is a new dynamic in the relations between church and state, or between religion and politics more generally. But they are also analytically separable.

It also helps to identify an interim phase between the two. Three categories of religious organization did not simply meld into two. Thinking of it in those terms causes us to miss the violence associated with any social change as basic as this one. Natural communities were torn asunder, their parts flung into the air and scattered in strange configurations, before the subterranean forces at work in the society finally rearranged them in the patterns we see today. We have to recognize the upheaval and displacement associated with this process if we are to tap the wellsprings from which much of the present political fury arises.

The erosion of the divisions separating Protestants and Catholics, Jews and Christians, and members of different denominations came about gradually. It was legitimated from within by norms of love and humility that promoted interfaith cooperation. It was reinforced from without by changes in the larger society. Rising educational levels, memories of the Holocaust, and the civil rights movement all contributed to an increasing emphasis on tolerance. Regional migration brought Catholics and Protestants, and Christians and Jews, into closer physical proximity with one another. Denominational ghettos, forged by immigration and ethnic ties, were gradually replaced by religiously and ethnically plural communities. Rates of interreligious marriage went up. It became increasingly common for members of all religious groups to have grown up in other groups, to have friends from other groups, and to have attended other groups.

The denominational hierarchies, seminaries, pension plans, and so forth still played a significant role in the organization of American religion. But the ground was in a sense cleared of old demarcations, thereby making new alliances and cleavages easier to emerge.

For those who had spent their entire lives within particular denominational ghettos, these changes in themselves represented major disruptions, of course, especially when it was their pastor who began welcoming outsiders, their denomination that lost its identity by merging with another, or their child who married outside the faith.

Most of the upheaval, though, came during the 1960s and was closely associated with the upheaval that pervaded the society in general. Young people were particularly subject to this upheaval. Many were the first ever in their families to attend college. For many, attending college meant leaving the ethno-religious ghetto for the first time. The campuses themselves were growing so rapidly that alienation and social isolation were common experiences. Of course, the civil rights movement and antiwar protests added to the turmoil.

Among the many ways in which this upheaval affected religion, two are especially important. First, the tensions of the 1960s significantly widened the gap between values and behavior that was mentioned earlier. The two major social movements of this period were the civil rights movement and the antiwar movement, and significantly, both dramatized the disjuncture between values and behavior. The civil rights movement brought into sharp relief what Gunnar Myrdal had called the "American dilemma"—the dilemma of subscribing to egalitarian values in principle but engaging in racial discrimination in practice.[11] Here was a clear example of values and behavior being out of joint.

The antiwar movement pointed up a similar disjuncture. On the one hand, Americans supposedly believed deeply in such values as democracy and the right of people to determine their own destiny. On the other hand, the country was engaged in a war in Southeast Asia that to many seemed to deny these principles. Military force was being used, at best, in an effort to determine another people's destiny

11. Gunnar Myrdal, *An American Dilemma* (New York: Harper & Brothers, 1944).

for them, or at worst, to prop up an ineffective nondemocratic regime. Both movements drove home, often implicitly, the more general point that people of high values and good consciences could not always be counted on to manifest those virtues in their day-to-day behavior.

The wedge that these movements drove into the earlier connection between values and behavior was to prove increasingly important in separating religious liberals from religious conservatives. Although this picture was to be modified somewhat by the 1980s, in the late 1960s it essentially consisted of conservatives grasping the values side of the equation and liberals seizing the behavioral side. That is, conservatives continued to emphasize preaching and teaching, the shaping of high personal moral standards, and above all the personally redemptive experience of salvation. Whether behavior would result that could alleviate racial discrimination or the war in Southeast Asia was not the issue; the issue was what one believed in one's heart and the motives from which one acted. In contrast, liberals increasingly attached importance to behavior. Believe what one will, it does not matter, they said, unless one puts one's faith on the line, takes action, helps bring about change. Changing social institutions was especially important, because they were the reason values and behavior did not correspond. People with good intentions were caught up in evil systems that needed to be overthrown.

For the time being at least, liberals argued for religious organizations' taking direct action in politics, while conservatives remained aloof from politics entirely, preferring instead to concentrate on matters of personal belief. Indeed, the two often gave lip service to the higher principles held by the other but expressed disagreement over the tactics being used. Thus, conservatives often expressed sympathy with the ideal of racial equality, but argued against the direct-action techniques in which liberal clergy were becoming involved. Liberals often continued to express sympathy with the ideal of personal salvation, but argued that personal salvation alone was not enough of a witness if church people did not become actively involved in working for social justice as well.

The second consequence of the turmoil of the 1960s that stands out is the increasing role of higher education in differentiating styles of religious commitment. In the 1950s, perhaps surprisingly so in retrospect, those who had been to college and those who had not were remarkably similar on most items of religious belief and practice. By the early 1970s, a considerable education gap had emerged between the two.

The college educated were much less likely, even than the college educated of the previous decade, to attend religious services regularly. Their belief in a literal interpretation of the Bible had eroded dramatically. They were more tolerant of other religions, and they were more interested in experimenting with the so-called new religions, such as Zen, Transcendental Meditation, Hare Krishna, and the human potential movement. Those who had not been to college remained more committed to traditional views of the Bible, were more strongly interested in religion in general, continued to attend religious services regularly, and expressed doubt about other faiths, including the new religions.

In short, educational differences were becoming more significant for religion, just as they were being emphasized more generally in the society. Higher education was becoming a more significant basis for creating social and cultural distinctions. In regard to religion, education was beginning to reinforce the cleavage between religious liberals and religious conservatives.

For a time, perhaps even as recently as 1976, it appeared that the gap between religious liberals and conservatives might be bridged by a significant segment of the evangelical community. Many of its leaders had participated in the educational expansion of the previous decade. They were exposed to the current thinking in higher education, had been influenced by their own participation in the civil rights movement and the antiwar movement, and had come to hold liberal views on many political issues, and yet retained a strong commitment to the biblical tradition, including an emphasis on personal faith.

Their voice, however, was soon drowned out by the more strident voices of the religious right. Television hookups and direct-mail solicitations replaced the evangelical periodical, seminary, and scholarly conference as more effective means of forging a large following and extracting revenue from that following. Issues such as abortion and feminism provided platforms on which the religious right could organize.

Educational differences continued to separate the more conservative from the more liberal. But other issues began to reinforce these differences. Issues arose that also reflected the experience of women in gaining higher education and becoming employed in professional careers, or the exposure one gained in college to the social sciences and humanities as opposed to more narrowly technical educations in engineering or business.

The religious right also borrowed the more activist style of political confrontation that the left had used during the 1960s. It began to renew the connection between values and behavior. Its commitment to personal morality remained strong, but it now urged believers to take political action, to organize themselves, to infuse their morality into the basic institutions of government. Each side developed special purpose groups to gain its objectives, either within more narrow denominational contexts or in the national arena.

Thus, deeper features of the social and cultural terrain underlie the present fracture between religious liberals and religious conservatives. Had it simply been, say, the Supreme Court's 1973 decision on abortion that elicited different responses from liberals and conservatives, we might well have seen a temporary flurry of activity followed by a gradual progression of interest to other matters. Instead, the religious environment is characterized by two clearly identified communities. Each has developed through the events spanning at least a quarter of a century. The two are located differently with respect to the basic social division that has been produced by the growth of higher education. Other bases of differentiation, such as regionalism, ethnicity, and denominationalism, that might have mitigated this basic division have subsided in importance. Each side has mobilized its resources around special purpose groups.

It is, therefore, highly likely that specific issues concerning the relations between church and state, cases in the federal courts involving religion, and religious issues in electoral campaigns will continue to evoke strong—and opposing—responses from these two communities.

FACTORS MITIGATING THE STRUGGLE

At the same time, we should not avoid mentioning several forces that may work to contain or reduce this polarization of religion in the public arena. One is the fact that neither community is actually organized as a single party. Each side is still divided into dozens of denominations, is represented by dozens of different national leaders, has mobilized its political efforts through dozens of special purpose groups, and at the grass roots consists of thousands of separate congregations. For either side to operate effectively as a political bloc, it must forge coalitions among these various organizations. And, despite the fact that both sides have been able to transcend old divisions, matters of theology, of liturgical tradition, and even of region still present formidable barriers to be overcome.

Another mitigating factor is that both sides continue to register,

at least at the grass roots, a healthy suspicion of government. It sometimes appears that each side is anxious to use government to achieve
its goals. But grass-roots mobilization of church people, whether
liberals or conservatives, has been more effective in opposing government than in cooperating with government.

During the civil rights movement, churchgoers who became
most active in politics at the grass roots were those who opposed the
actions being taken by the government. During the Vietnam War,
churchgoers most active in politics were again those who opposed the
government's actions. In recent years, the most politically active
churchgoers have been those who opposed the government's role on
abortion and welfare spending. In each of these periods, moreover,
churchgoers who felt government was becoming too powerful were
more likely to become politically active than churchgoers who did not
feel this way. I suspect that the reason for this political activism lies in
the fact that there is a long history of concern, expressed specifically
in the First Amendment to the Constitution, over the threat that
government poses to religious freedom. In any case, this suspicion of
government seems likely to dampen enthusiasm for any strong theo-
cratic orientation of the kind that has sometimes been projected.

Finally, we must remember that the involvement of either
religious faction in political life cannot succeed without active support
from leaders in the political arena itself. During the 1980s, under the
Reagan administration, at least an impression of such support was often
taken for granted. At the same time, officials of both political parties
have often expressed consternation over the activities of religious
groups. Lack of political experience, extremist rhetoric, disinterest in
routine party activities, and single-issue orientations have been cited
as reasons for this consternation.

Moreover, religious liberals and religious conservatives have
often been courted by factions within the political community for entirely secular purposes: because they supported stronger defense initiatives, or because they favored a freeze on nuclear weapons, or because they wanted a tougher policy against communism in Latin
America. Either military or economic changes in the larger international arena can radically alter the nature of these issues, and therefore the
likelihood of religious factions being courted.

I return, then, to the point at which I began. The relations between faith and politics are contingent on the broader terrain on which
they occur. Like the Battle of Waterloo, the battle between religious
conservatives and religious liberals is subject to its environment. A

deep cultural ravine appears to separate the two communities. Whether this ravine can be bridged depends on raising it from obscurity, bringing it into consciousness, and recognizing the surrounding contours on which these efforts must rest.

Three   Contested Terrain

No personal devotional confrontation?

ONLY IN THE PRACTICAL, AND OFTEN DIFFICULT, attempt to relate our religious faith to public affairs do our theologies acquire meaning. And only within the cultural, economic, political, and religious contexts of our collective experience do these meanings gain tangible expression. Thus we must understand the broader social context, and not simply the internal logic of our religious doctrines, if we are to grasp their contemporary and future significance.

Yet the broader social context in which the relations between religion and public affairs are defined is itself in constant flux. Two centuries ago, when the First Amendment religious clauses were formulated, fears of an established state church of the kind existing in England figured prominently in the public mind. As recently as the late 1940s, Protestant leaders actively championed strict separation of church and state because they feared Catholics were maneuvering to gain special concessions for themselves through legal and judicial action. Today, these expressions of fear seem strikingly out of place. But other conditions, both within American religion and in the broader society, have combined to arouse new concerns about the role of faith in public affairs. What, then, must we understand about the present social situation in order to deepen our appreciation of the distinctive relations between faith and public life in the American context?

If there is currently a struggle for America's soul, why has this

39

struggle taken on the proportions it has? Why has the division between evangelical and liberal Christians ruptured into a dispute that we all read about and see enacted on the evening news? Why is each faction making such aggressive claims on the public character of our society?

The complexities involved in trying to answer these questions can be illustrated by an op-ed article that appeared in the *New York Times*. The author argued that political liberals should imitate political conservatives in making better use of religious groups and religious appeals in promoting their agenda. She urged that churches and synagogues should be used more effectively to "instill a commitment to social goals, focus on local issues and mobilize a nationwide movement." Religious traditions should be examined to find "models for strength and compassion." If liberals remained unwilling to explore the religious heritage in American culture, she warned, then "the religious traditions of an entire nation" would have been surrendered to their opponents, and the nation might well be led "in a direction repugnant to all those who insist on the human rights and dignity of each individual."[1]

To this writer—a Boston lawyer—the religion clauses of the First Amendment served as implicit guidelines for framing arguments about the role of religion in contemporary political affairs. In her view, religious groups should remain strictly separated from the state: influencing the public sphere only by reinforcing individual concerns, disseminating information, and letting political action committees take the lead in organizing direct-mail efforts and campaign activities. At the same time, she argued, the freedom of all religious groups to state their views on public issues should be respected, even encouraged, as a way of bringing pluralism into the public arena.

Within these broad, implicit guidelines, the specific ways in which religious faith should be related to the public sphere nevertheless remained, for this writer, dependent on the unique social and cultural conditions of the period. Uppermost in her mind was an apparent division between liberals and conservatives—a division that had religious as well as political dimensions. Issues of health care and shelter, personal responsibility, justice, excessive disparities of wealth, degradation of women, and human rights provided the operative definitions of a liberal politico-religious orientation. Images of freedom, tolerance, virtue, the poor and the meek, weapons and plowshares

NoT Bad !

1. Kathleen Kennedy Townsend, "The Bible and the Left," *New York Times*, 9 August 1981.

provided substance to the author's call to recapture the biblical tradition. Movements, political action committees, direct-mail campaigns, and lobbying provided the framework in which participation in the public sphere was described. All of these features of this writer's discourse reflected the broader conditions shaping her understanding of how faith should be related to public affairs.

In broad outline, I shall in this chapter examine several of the social developments in American society that have been regarded as significant features of the cultural context in which recent debates about the public role of religion have been framed. I shall try to suggest, by examining briefly some of the relevant evidence, that a few of these arguments have been overstated (or are simply wrong), while other arguments of potential importance have not been emphasized enough. Having considered these arguments about the broader contexts conditioning contemporary understandings of religion's role in public affairs, we shall then be in a position to consider some of the implications of the ways in which these understandings are presently structured.

Beyond the specific issues that are debated most contentiously, there are, I believe, significant implications for American religion itself and for the ways in which we define civic responsibility. Before these issues can be considered, however, we must attempt to say more clearly what the contemporary debates are and to identify the major contestants in these debates.

CONTESTED ISSUES

At first glance, the issues that have drawn religious groups into the public sphere in recent years are bewilderingly diverse. Nuclear arms negotiations, the sale of infant formula to mothers in the Third World, aid to Contra rebels in Nicaragua, an Equal Rights Amendment to the Constitution, military and economic policy in the Middle East, prayer in public schools, Internal Revenue Service policies toward religious broadcasters, abortion, nominations to the Supreme Court, and a host of other issues have all been the subject of intense discussion, and often of activism as well, by religious groups of all kinds.

Much of this activism has precedent: in the role of religious groups in the abolitionist movement, the movement to ratify (and later to repeal) Prohibition, and the civil rights movement. Unlike these earlier episodes, however, the issues currently evoking religious participation appear to be greater in number, and (perhaps for this reason) draw responses from a wider range of denominations and faiths. Indeed, our public philosophy has been enriched greatly by the dizzying array of religious perspectives that have been brought to bear on contemporary issues.

Closer inspection indicates that the pattern of responses is not as bewildering as it might at first appear. Some issues are consistently supported by certain segments of the religious community and are consistently opposed by other segments of this community. In fact, empirical studies, based on analyses of public opinion surveys, suggest a kind of polarization among the American people around a number of issues. For instance, a study published in 1983 showed that opponents of the Supreme Court's ruling against prayer in public schools tended to coincide with opponents of abortion, with opponents of homosexuality, and with opponents of greater equality for women. Supporters on each of these issues tended to cluster into a separate category.[2]

Data collected by the Gallup Organization in 1984 also suggested that religious liberals tend to be polarized from religious conservatives on many of these issues. For instance, three times as many religious conservatives as religious liberals said they were strongly opposed to abortion on demand. Twice as many religious conservatives as religious liberals said they strongly favored voluntary prayer in schools. On the other side, more government spending on social programs and unilateral nuclear disarmament received support from about twice as many religious liberals as religious conservatives.[3]

These kinds of evidence give some support for the idea—made popular by media reports—that religious fundamentalists are lined up on one side of most issues, and that they are opposed by secular humanists. The actual situation is much more complex.

For instance, on the fundamentalist side are groups that strongly resist all efforts to be dragged into political controversies. There are divisions between old-line fundamentalists, who still make white supremacy and McCarthyite anticommunism their main social appeals, and newer fundamentalist groups that stake their reputations on pro-

2. See John H. Simpson, "Moral Issues and Status Politics," in *The New Christian Right: Mobilization and Legitimation*, ed. Robert C. Liebman and Robert Wuthnow (New York: Aldine, 1983), pp. 187-205.

3. Gallup Organization, "How Can Christian Liberals and Conservatives Be Brought Together?" (Unpublished report, 1984). Further analyses of these and other data are reported in Robert Wuthnow, *The Restructuring of American Religion: Society and Faith Since World War II* (Princeton: Princeton University Press, 1988).

life advocacy. Fundamentalists and evangelicals are also sharply divided: not only on the degree of literalness with which they interpret the Bible, but also on questions of civil liberties and social programs. Some evangelical groups have even championed so-called liberal causes such as nuclear disarmament, gender equality, and government programs for the poor.

At the opposite extreme, those whom fundamentalist activists sometimes label secular humanists also defy easy categorization. Militant humanists appear to constitute an extremely small segment of the population, while many others who may distance themselves from fundamentalism still retain some identification with mainstream Protestant churches (or with Catholicism or Judaism), or have adopted a more personalized variety of faith.

If one took into account the full variety of denominations, religious interest groups, and quasi-religious groups that have expressed views on public issues of one kind or another, the range of opinions and understandings would indeed be immense. Virtually every point of view—from ones arguing explicitly for the establishment of Christianity as a national religion to ones favoring the complete eradication of religion from all public affairs, with nearly every conceivable position in between—has been articulated. Yet the same polarization that seems evident on specific issues runs through the more general debate over the proper relation of faith to the public sphere.

The labels that the media have taught the public itself to use— "religious liberals" and "religious conservatives"—have become symbolic of different understandings of how best to relate religion and public affairs. Liberalism in religion has come to be associated with taking a strong stand on the establishment clause in our Constitution; conservatism, with placing greater emphasis on the right to free expression of religion. The former view, as it has been worked out operationally in recent decades, has tended to worry most about religious groups (usually ones sympathizing with conservative political and economic causes) using the several branches of the government to gain unfair advantage for their preferred interests. The latter view—emphasizing free expression—has been more concerned about an apparent tendency within government and among other ruling elites to squeeze religion out of the public sphere entirely.

Underlying the debate between these two positions is a great deal of common conceptual ground, and indeed much diversity of interpretation on specific issues—diversity and agreement that is often

overshadowed by the intensity of conflict between liberals and conservatives. For instance, when pressed, liberal religious leaders give
strong support to the idea of free expression and even recognize that
their own efforts (e.g., to promote nuclear disarmament) constitute collective intervention by religious groups in the public sphere. When
conservative religious leaders are questioned, they generally shy away
from anything resembling an actual establishment of religion, speak
out strongly in favor of religious pluralism, and draw subtle distinctions between their religious beliefs and the politics of public morality.

It is for this reason that the charges and countercharges that
religious factions hurl back and forth at each other often sound
hypocritical. For example, liberals complain that conservatives are
dragging personal morality into the public arena by calling for legislation against abortion. Yet they themselves stand behind court decisions
that are very much efforts by the government to say what is, and what
is not, personal morality. For their part, conservatives accuse liberals
of selling out the country to secular humanism, but fail to recognize
the deeply religious convictions from which liberals may take their
stands on peace, social justice, or strict separation of church and state.

What has perplexed many observers of this conflict in recent
years is that neither side seems to be able to speak persuasively to the
other. That is, despite many shared assumptions—and despite crosscutting loyalties embedded within the historic diversity of American
religion—neither side seems to be able to communicate effectively
with the other.

In his widely read book *After Virtue*, Alasdair MacIntyre has
shown that on issues such as abortion and nuclear weapons different
sides seem to be able to articulate perfectly rational and logical arguments that can be traced consistently to certain basic premises. But
then neither side can find a way to bridge into the premises of the
other. Stalemate is the result.[4] In practice, different religio-political factions organize around these differing premises, draw in constituents
who somehow feel intuitively comfortable with their basic premises,
take different sides on controversial issues, but seldom find any way
of resolving these issues.

In her book *Abortion and the Politics of Motherhood*, sociologist
Kristin Luker has shown that pro-life and pro-choice activists do not
differ from one another simply on the question of abortion. They dif-

---

4. Alasdair MacIntyre, *After Virtue* (South Bend, IN: University of Notre Dame
Press, 1981).

fer fundamentally, she argues, on such basic premises about family and religious values, careers, gender, one's body, personal rights, and social responsibilities that little basis is left for communication.[5] Luker's study seems to apply to many other issues as well. In debating the proper role of religion—or of absolute values in general—in public affairs, we seem to run into such fundamental disagreements that communication itself comes to an impasse. Why?

MacIntyre suggests that the problem is philosophical. We have, he believes, lost sight of so many of the puzzle pieces with which the founders of modern civilization constructed philosophical arguments that we can no longer create a coherent picture. Thus, we arrive in our deliberations at different sections of the puzzle and somehow convince ourselves that we have seen the whole puzzle. But in reality, MacIntyre claims, we have only seen part of the puzzle. We must rediscover some important transcendent beliefs about the nature of God and the world if we are to communicate effectively about the dilemmas confronting us in public life.

But this argument is itself incomplete. At least to the sociologically minded, it rings of talk about disembodied ideas and fails to recognize the institutional realities in which ideas are embedded. Luker, as a sociologist, comes closer to emphasizing some of these institutional realities when she considers the effects of childhood training, marriage, and careers on pro-life and pro-choice activists. Her analysis is of limited value, however, because of its focus on the distinctive contexts in which these activists function. In order to grasp the larger contexts in which contemporary debates about religion's relation to public affairs are situated, we need to consider a different set of arguments.

THE CONTEXTS OF CONTROVERSY

Social scientists, journalists, and religious leaders have all sought to provide explanations—many of which have in fact focused on institutional realities—for the contemporary controversies concerning the role of religion in public life. It has been difficult to formulate arguments that fully accord with the evidence at our disposal, however, because the very nature of this evidence is highly unstable. Year by

5. Kristin Luker, *Abortion and the Politics of Motherhood* (Berkeley and Los Angeles: University of California Press, 1984).

year the issues themselves have changed, the fortunes of the various
protagonists have been affected by changing circumstances (and sometimes by personalities as well), and new studies continually alter our
perceptions of dominant trends. What we can say, therefore, must always be contingent on the period in which it is said.

Religious Revival

The argument that has perhaps been touted most frequently in popular accounts of current controversies over the role of religion in American public life is the idea that these controversies have been reinforced by a revival of religious sentiment. According to this argument,
religion has begun flexing its muscles, and in so doing, it is trying to
move the boundaries between church and state. Like the problems in
Iran and Northern Ireland, the controversies in the United States are
attributed to a resurgence of militant religion, especially fundamentalism.

According to some interpreters, this religious revival is a kind
of temporary throwback. Modernity has generated its discontents. A
return to religion has been the answer. Over the long haul, secularization will melt away this reservoir of discontent. But in the meantime,
religious people can be expected to cause trouble.

Others view the contemporary revival more as a rediscovery
of something important in the American tradition. During much of the
twentieth century, they argue, people were preoccupied with the pur-
suit of material comfort. Once that had been achieved, at least for the
vast majority, the inability of prosperity alone to provide meaning in
life became apparent. The complacent 1950s were thus succeeded by
the turbulent 1960s—a time when people explored everything from
drugs to political activism in a desperate effort to discover meaning.
Those explorations, too, produced little more than discontent, and an
increasing number of counterculture activists turned to religion. As
the 1970s brought a more politically settled milieu, larger segments of
the population in general also began turning back to the churches and
synagogues. The result was the increased concern about the public
role of religion that became evident in the 1980s.

These are admittedly caricatures of more complex arguments.
Whatever the specific views of religious revival that are cited, though,
they rest ultimately on the assumption that a religious revival has indeed taken place. But that assumption itself needs to be scrutinized.

Thanks to the efforts of pollsters, the pulse of American religion has been taken repeatedly in recent years to see if it is beating more rapidly than in the past. These measures often lack sophistication and depth, but they do provide general benchmarks, and enough analyses of these benchmarks have been done to verify their relation to more sophisticated indicators of religious commitment.

The standard measures of religious commitment give very little support to the idea of a religious revival having taken place in recent years. For instance, studies of attendance at religious services conducted in 1987 showed that the percentage of adults in the United States who said they had attended church or synagogue in the last seven days was no greater than it had been in other years; indeed, the level of churchgoing had not changed significantly since 1969.[6] Studies of membership in churches and synagogues also reveal no evidence of a religious revival: the proportion indicating membership has varied between 67 percent and 71 percent for more than a decade.[7]

These indicators may be limited because they focus on participation in organized religion. Indeed, many observers have speculated that religion may be turning in a less organized, more private (but still influential) direction. But even a relatively subjective question such as "How important would you say religion is in your life?" shows little change in recent years: the proportion responding "very important" has remained constant (at about 55 percent) for the past decade.[8]

Other kinds of indicators suggest that religious commitment may be declining rather than experiencing a revival. For example, the proportion of the public expressing confidence in the church or organized religion dropped from 66 percent in 1973 to 62 percent in 1982, and then to 54 percent in 1987.[9]

Some evidence of declining commitment to religion is also present in responses to the question "Can religion answer all or most of today's problems?" In 1957, 81 percent of the American public said yes. By 1974 this figure had dropped to 62 percent, and by 1986 it had eroded further to 57 percent.[10] Even in an area in which religion has

6. These figures are from Gallup surveys. The figure for 1987 was 40 percent. Other figures reported for years between 1969 and 1987 varied between 40 percent and 42 percent. See *Emerging Trends*, November 1987, p. 5. *Emerging Trends* is a monthly publication of the Princeton Religion Research Center, an affiliate of the Gallup Organization in Princeton, New Jersey.

7. *Emerging Trends*, January 1987, p. 2.

8. Ibid., p. 6.

9. *Emerging Trends*, April 1987, p. 1.

10. *Emerging Trends*, November-December 1986, p. 8.

generally been thought to exercise an especially powerful influence—strengthening the family—fewer of the public now say religion has been effective than did only a short time ago.[11]

Thus, on the whole, many people seem to feel the society is becoming more secular rather than more religious. For instance, in 1988, 49 percent of the public felt religion was losing influence in America, while only 36 percent thought it was gaining influence.[12] But a fair reading of the arguments about religious revival does not suggest that religion of all kinds should be on the upswing—only that fundamentalists and evangelicals are for some reason becoming more numerous.[13] Here too public opinion surveys provide some useful statistics, though again, these surveys do not seem to support the idea of a religious revival.

For example, membership statistics reported by some evangelical and fundamentalist denominations suggest spectacular growth. Denominations such as the Assemblies of God, Evangelical Free, and Independent Baptists have grown at rates exceeding that of the general population, while older denominations (Episcopalian, Presbyterian, Methodist) have generally experienced membership declines.[14] Most of these denominations remain small, however, both in absolute terms and relative to the larger number of people in the United States who consider themselves fundamentalists or evangelicals.

Survey studies that ask about religious self-definitions and about the kinds of beliefs that are generally associated with evangelicalism or fundamentalism suggest no increases in numeric strength overall. For example, measures used by the Gallup Organization and by the University of Michigan's National Election Surveys find consistently that about 12 or 13 percent of the public can be considered fundamentalist or evangelical in terms of their religious views, and these

---

11. Between 1980 and 1986 the percentage who said religion had strengthened their family relationships a great deal declined from 39 percent to 35 percent, while those who said religion had strengthened family relations hardly at all or not at all increased from 23 percent to 26 percent. Reported in *Emerging Trends*, January 1987, p. 4.

12. *Emerging Trends*, March 1988, p. 1.

13. The terms "fundamentalist" and "evangelical" have historic connotations that are often neglected in surveys and in discussions in the media. At present, those groups and individuals who use the term "fundamentalist" tend to place strong emphasis on the divine verbal inspiration and absolute inerrancy of the Bible, while "evangelicals" maintain that the Bible is divinely inspired but may take a more figurative interpretation of some of its content.

14. See Wuthnow, *Restructuring of American Religion*, especially chapters 7 and 8.

figures have remained constant since the mid-1970s when they were first used.[15]

Less direct measures indicate much the same conclusion. For instance, one might consider daily Bible reading a sign of strong traditional religious commitment, even if Bible readers did not apply the label fundamentalist to themselves. But polls that have examined Bible reading give no sign of an upsurge in this activity: in 1978, 12 percent of the public said they read the Bible daily; in 1986, the figure was 11 percent.[16]

If the percentage of the population that in some way associates itself with fundamentalism or fundamentalist beliefs has neither increased nor decreased, polls asking representative samples of the entire public what they think of evangelicals and fundamentalists suggest an actual *decrease* in tolerance of these groups. For example, studies of voter preferences showed that voters in 1980 were more likely to vote for a candidate who was a born-again evangelical Christian; but by 1987, voters were *less likely* to vote for a self-proclaimed evangelical.[17]

Over the same period—reflecting reactions to the highly publicized sex scandals involving television evangelists Jim Bakker and Jimmy Swaggart—attitudes toward evangelical leaders also turned increasingly unfavorable. For instance, 63 percent of the public said television evangelists were untrustworthy with money, compared with only 36 percent who had given the same response in 1980. Favorable ratings of major evangelical television personalities—Oral Roberts, Jimmy Swaggart, Pat Robertson, Robert Schuller, Rex Humbard— declined significantly.[18]

Outright intolerance of the fundamentalist rank and file itself is limited to relatively small segments of the population. But again, some evidence of increasing intolerance has been found. In comparison with intolerance toward more traditional targets of religious hostility, such as Catholics or Jews, the percentages expressing negative attitudes toward fundamentalists are relatively high.[19]

15. Ibid., especially chapter 8.
16. *Emerging Trends,* November-December 1986, p. 6.
17. The 1980 figures were 19 percent "more likely" compared with 9 percent "less likely"; the 1987 figures were 15 percent "more likely" compared with 29 percent "less likely." These figures are reported in *Emerging Trends,* April 1987, p. 5.
18. Ibid.
19. National surveys conducted in 1981 and again in 1987 showed, respectively, that 11 percent and 13 percent of the public would not like to have fundamentalists as neighbors; the proportions expressing similar attitudes toward Catholics and Jews, respectively, were 1 percent and 2 percent in 1981, and 1 percent and 3 percent in 1987. Reported in *Emerging Trends,* March 1987, p. 1.

If polls and surveys fail to turn up evidence of a religious revival, they do nevertheless tell us one thing that we must always remember in considering the public role of American religion: in comparison with other countries, religious commitment in the United States remains at a very high level. For example, a multinational survey in 1981 asked respondents in a number of countries to rate the importance of God in their lives on a ten-point scale. Respondents in the United States averaged 8.21 in their ratings. In comparison, respondents in Great Britain averaged 5.72; in West Germany, 5.67; in Japan, 4.83; in France, 4.72; and in Sweden, 3.99. Another question in the same study asked respondents to say whether they considered themselves "a religious person." In the United States, 83 percent did, compared with an average of only 66 percent in 14 other countries.[20]

Whether a question like this one has meaning is open to debate. But other studies—and indeed other kinds of evidence—also point to the exceptional levels of religiosity in the United States compared with other advanced industrial societies. For instance, three times as many young people in the United States say they include religious activities in their typical weekend events than in Great Britain, West Germany, or France. In the United States, the number of Bibles purchased annually per capita is more than double that in Great Britain, nearly five times as high as in West Germany, and eleven times the number in France. In the United States, one church exists for approximately every 500 people, whereas in each of the other three countries one church exists for only every 1,000 members of the population. Clergy per capita in the United States exceeds that in Great Britain and West Germany by a ratio of two to one (and is marginally higher than in France).[21]

20. These figures are from a forthcoming book by Ronald Inglehart, Professor of Political Science at the University of Michigan, which is to be published by Princeton University Press. His analysis of these data also suggests that secularization among young people may be taking place more rapidly in other countries than in the United States. For instance, among respondents age 65 and over, the mean figure for 15 countries was only 10 percentage points lower than the figure for the United States. But among respondents age 25 to 34, there was a 20 point difference; and among respondents age 15 to 24, the gap was 22 points. He notes the difficulties in inferring cultural trends from comparing age groups. I wish to thank Professor Inglehart for making preliminary drafts of sections of his book available to me.

21. These figures are calculated from evidence reported in recent volumes of census statistics for each country. Another powerful indication of the United States' exceptionalism on matters religious comes from an attempt by political scientist Kenneth D. Wald to say how much the United States deviates from the pattern one would expect from correlating religiosity with an index of economic development. Drawing on data

Bearing in mind the importance of religious commitment to large segments of the American population helps, at least in a general way, to make sense of the intensity with which questions about religion's role in public affairs are debated. Simply put, religion is extremely salient. There is a threshold of interest that makes it more of a factor in our public debates than in many other advanced industrial societies. The fact that this interest has remained at such high levels does not account for the more specific controversies that have arisen in recent years. It does, however, serve as one of the preconditions of the broader context in which these controversies have emerged.

Religious Mobilization

If a revival in the sheer level of religious commitment cannot be adduced convincingly to explain changes in the public role of American religion, a somewhat more nuanced argument can be developed by paying attention to the ways in which religious sentiments are mobilized. There are many indications that religious people have become organized to participate in public affairs more effectively.

Until fairly recently, the dominant ways in which religious people participated in public affairs consisted of activities sponsored at the national or regional levels by denominations, activities sponsored at the local level by local churches and synagogues, and activities organized by secular groups in which persons with religious convictions took part as private individuals. In the 1980s, all these modes of public participation could still be seen among religious people. But an important new form of organization also arose: the special purpose group.

Organized to accomplish explicitly focused objectives, the special purpose group differs dramatically from all of the more familiar modes of participation in public affairs. Unlike denominations, special purpose groups are able to devote their energies to a more limited array of activities. They do not have to concern themselves with building and staffing churches, with running seminaries, or with rendering

---

from more than a dozen countries, Wald was able to establish a strong negative correlation between economic development and the likelihood of survey respondents to consider religion important. So strong was this tendency, in fact, that in the United States only 5 percent of the public should regard religion as important—if the United States were like other countries. But in fact, 51 percent said they considered religion important. See Kenneth D. Wald, *Religion and Politics in the United States* (New York: St. Martin's Press, 1987), p. 7.

doctrinal interpretations. Freed from the historical and theological legacies that have separated denominations, special purpose groups have also been able to draw supporters from a wide range of religious traditions. Some have even managed to garner support from Catholics and Jews in addition to members of various Protestant denominations.

Unlike the local church or synagogue, special purpose groups have the advantage of operating on a national scale. They can draw contributions from all parts of the country, and then channel these resources toward lobbying efforts in the nation's capital, or toward selected regional issues. In contrast to local churches and synagogues, they also enjoy greater flexibility. As issues change, their appeals can change accordingly, whereas local congregations are generally committed to a wider range of services for their parishioners.

Unlike the activities that persons with religious convictions may participate in as private individuals, these special purpose groups give explicit identity to religious and religio-moral issues. They provide a way in which individuals can reinforce one another, not simply as members of some political party or secular action group, but as persons with common religious convictions. In so doing, they also make religious convictions more visible in the public arena. No longer is it merely private conscience that influences our public philosophy, but the organized activities of a religious collectivity.

Over the past decade, the most widely discussed religious special purpose group has probably been televangelist Jerry Falwell's organization, popularly known as Moral Majority, or following a 1985 reorganization, the Liberty Federation. All of the distinctive organizational features of special purpose groups just mentioned can be seen in this organization. It has been able to draw support from a wide spectrum of religious conservatives. It has focused on a limited set of public issues, such as abortion and the Equal Rights Amendment, giving priority to different issues as political expediency dictated, rather than offering a full range of theological and ecclesiastical services. Indeed, it has circumvented restrictions on religious groups' participation in political affairs by specifically denying that it is a religious organization. It has also greatly extended the political reach of Falwell's local church in Lynchburg, Virginia. With national broadcasting facilities it has been able to raise money from donors throughout the United States and to address national issues. It has provided a conduit for channeling excess funds from Falwell's church into political activities, and at other times has channeled money raised for political purposes (though a complex lending arrangement) into Falwell's many religious organizations. It has also been a very significant factor in the visibility that religious conservatives have gained as a collective entity in American politics.

Because many special purpose groups lead ephemeral lives, it has been difficult for social observers to determine how extensive their activities may have become. These problems are compounded in the case of religious special purpose groups because of relatively lax legal and financial reporting requirements. Nevertheless, the available evidence points clearly to the fact that these kinds of organizations have grown both in numbers and in political significance. For instance, one estimate suggests that by the mid-1980s more than 800 religious special purpose groups had been organized as national nonprofit organizations—with more than half of these organizations coming into existence since the early 1960s—and that as many as one adult in five claimed to hold membership in one or more of these organizations.[22]

A number of factors have contributed to the growth of these special purpose groups. Religious television has played an important role in some of them. It has provided the critical link between leaders interested in exercising greater influence in the public arena and a national grass-roots constituency. Cable television hookups and computerized direct-mail technologies have also played this role. Another contributing factor has been the growth of secular special purpose groups. Religious organizers have often imitated more established organizations, such as the American Civil Liberties Union, Common Cause, and the League of Women Voters. During the 1960s and early 1970s, the number of these organizations grew rapidly, especially those that concerned themselves with issues relating to racial and gender equality and direct social action, and religious groups increasingly began initiating counterpart organizations for their own constituencies.

Within the religious community itself, ecumenical tendencies and greater interaction across denominational boundaries have been conducive to the growth of special purpose groups. For example, both the National Council of Churches and the National Association of Evangelicals have benefited from these tendencies and have facilitated other, more focused special purpose groups. As denominations have merged, forming larger and more diverse units, special purpose groups have also emerged as ways in which more homogeneous constituencies could express their interests at the denominational level.

More generally, the growth of special purpose groups has been

22. For additional detail, see Wuthnow, *Restructuring of American Religion,* especially chapter 6.

facilitated by the relatively high levels of economic prosperity and political freedom that have characterized the American environment. Their numbers have also grown as a product of the pluralism characteristic of American religion. Issues such as the Equal Rights Amendment, gay activism, and racial equality have generated special purpose groups not simply from religion in general but from Presbyterians, Mormons, Baptists, Catholics, Jews, and so on.

The political impact of special purpose groups has been especially significant among evangelicals and fundamentalists. Studies of grass-roots participation in electoral campaign activities prior to the mid-1970s generally showed that churchgoers of all kinds tended to be more actively involved than those who did not attend church, but that members of evangelical churches did not participate in political activities as often as members of more liberal Protestant and Catholic churches. In more recent presidential elections, though, only churchgoers who have conservative political interests have been more likely than nonattenders to participate in campaign activities, and on the whole, evangelicals and fundamentalists tend to be more politically active than religious liberals.[23]

The fact that religious communities have become better mobilized to participate in public affairs—through special purpose groups and other organizations—helps to account for the disparity (noted earlier) between the public's perception of religious influence in the United States and indicators of actual trends in religious sentiments. The sentiments have not changed—or at least do not suggest an across-the-board religious revival. Nor has the American public become more active in traditional kinds of religious groups. But those with strong religious convictions do appear to be better mobilized than ever before.

In a sense, then, religion's influence may have been increasing. At least religious groups are making more collective efforts now to influence the public sphere than they did only a few decades ago. Many of these efforts have been spearheaded by special purpose groups organized specifically for lobbying, registering voters, supporting candidates, and other political activities. Though the effectiveness of these efforts has often been questioned, the efforts themselves have received sufficient publicity to give an impression of renewed vitality within the religious community.

23. For a discussion of these findings, largely from my analyses of national surveys conducted by the Center for Political Studies at the University of Michigan, see ibid., especially chapters 8, 9, and 12.

A Liberal Court

If, on balance, religious groups have more organizational muscle than they did twenty or thirty years ago, the question still remains as to why this muscle has been flexed in certain directions and not others, as does the broader question of how this muscle flexing has influenced understandings of the relations between faith and public affairs. Religious groups have generally not operated in a political vacuum. As I have suggested, they have organized to accomplish specific objectives. They felt compelled to organize because these objectives were perceived to be in danger. An enemy had arisen with whom it was necessary to engage in combat.

That enemy was the Supreme Court. Its actions were increasingly interpreted as being antagonistic to the values that religious groups held dear. If the nation's moral strength was to be preserved, quick and effective action had to be taken to bring pressure on the Supreme Court to reverse some of its decisions, to subject the justices to such an outcry from the heartland that they could no longer ignore the wishes of the population, and if necessary to accomplish through legislation and executive mandate what could not be gained by challenging the judiciary.

The Court's significance had been driven home to many religious constituents in the late 1960s by its ruling against prayer in public schools and by its decision on abortion in 1973. Some members of conservative Protestant and Catholic churches began to mobilize opposition to the Court soon after these decisions were announced.

Over the following fifteen years the Court's involvement in cases concerning religion became even more evident. Decisions came down concerning the role of religious convictions in the workplace, the use of state funds for chaplains, church schools' and colleges' conformity to standards of racial equality, the use of government money for students attending parochial schools, and even such seemingly trivial matters as the posting of the Ten Commandments in public places and the printing of a "motorist's prayer" on state maps. In many of these decisions the Court took a hard line against religious practices of any kind receiving support from the state or even being allowed to enter into the political or economic realms.

By the 1980s many religious leaders had come to view the Supreme Court both as a determined foe of the specific positions on issues that religious conservatives championed and as a threat to long-cherished understandings of the First Amendment religion clauses themselves. Jerry Falwell asserted flatly that the Court's liberal views had established unconstitutional rights "to kill the unborn, commit homosexual acts, repress religious freedoms, [and] exploit women and children through pornographic publications."[24] Robert Grant, chairman of Christian Voice, urged his supporters to "return the law of our land to godly foundations while we have a chance."[25]

Expressing similar dismay at the orientation of the Court, Martha Rountree, head of the Leadership Foundation, wrote of her anger and disgust that "America's children can legally get birth control, sex books, and indecent literature in our schools, but can't legally pray, read the Bible, or have religious meetings there." She argued that the underlying problem was a "Supreme Court disaster" brought about by "liberal Federal judges." The only remaining solution to this problem was to "take away the power of the Supreme Court and other Federal judges to rule on issues involving school prayer, Bible reading and religious meetings."[26]

Whether the Court had in fact created a new understanding of the relations between church and state has been widely discussed, of course. The view that significant modifications in these relations have been implied by the Court has not been limited only to conservative religious leaders. Scholars attempting to assess the situation from an unbiased perspective have also arrived at this conclusion.

For example, political scientist Kenneth Wald observes that the Supreme Court has departed from previous interpretations of the First Amendment religious clauses in three important respects. It has applied the same standards governing federal policies toward religion to the state and local levels, thereby altering the practices of many communities. It has broadened the list of government actions that are construed as constituting an impermissible establishment of religion. And it has struck down an increasing number of practices that seemed to force individuals to endorse religious beliefs that might be contrary to their own.[27]

Viewing these changes in interpretation more generally, other scholars have also concluded that the Court has significantly modified the original intent of the framers of the Constitution and have departed from the way in which the religious clauses were interpreted until re-

24. Jerry Falwell, "A Chance to End Abortion," *Liberty Report,* August 1987, p. 2.
25. A direct-mail solicitation quoted in Kenneth B. Noble, "Bork Backers Flood Senate with Mail," *New York Times,* 3 September 1987.
26. From a 1987 direct-mail solicitation from the Leadership Foundation.
27. Wald, *Religion and Politics in the United States,* p. 116.

cently. Definitions of religion itself have become sufficiently ambiguous to render difficult any legally binding distinctions between church and nonchurch. Claims of conscience, rather than of formally recognized faith, continue to plague the courts for guarantees of free expression.[28]

Particularly at issue has been the widening wall of separation between religion and politics—a wall that some feel genuinely threatens the freedom of people with religious convictions to express those convictions in public arenas. As one writer has noted, the recent changes in interpretation by the Supreme Court have left many believers feeling that "the lifeblood of our religious freedom is slowly being sucked from our constitutionally protected veins."[29]

It may be, therefore, that some of the present debate over the proper role of religion in the public sphere has been generated by the Supreme Court itself. As the wall of separation between church and state has been restructured, religious groups have found themselves in opposition to the Court's interpretations and have mobilized accordingly, only to discover that this very mobilization evoked further responses from the Court. In the process, uncertainties about the underlying principles concerning church-state relations have also been allowed to surface. In view of the high levels of religious conviction present in the United States, it has not been surprising to see religious groups becoming increasingly active in trying to resolve these uncertainties.

To attribute the recent controversies primarily to a liberal Supreme Court, though, clearly does not address some of the broader aspects of these controversies that must also be understood. For example, it does not take into account the ways in which other activities of the government have contributed to these controversies. Nor does it give adequate recognition to the fact that in nearly every major case involving church-state issues some religious groups have supported the Court's interpretations while other religious groups have opposed the Court.

State Expansion

Over the past century—and especially since World War II—the activities of the federal government have expanded enormously. We have only to remind ourselves that standard time zones, uniform criminal

28. These changes are discussed in Phillip E. Hammond, "The Shifting Meaning of a Wall of Separation: Some Notes on Church, State, and Conscience," *Sociological Analysis* 42 (1981): 227-34.

29. Terry Muck, "The Wall That Never Was," *Christianity Today* (July 10, 1987): 16.

codes, Social Security numbers, centralized bank deposit insurance, federal regulation of the communications industry, a national system of food and drug regulations, and government supervision of fairness in employment and housing are all inventions of the twentieth century. Add to this expansion a 250 percent increase in government employment, a threefold increase in federal income taxes (after inflation), and a fourfold rise in the number of federal court cases since World War II, and it becomes obvious that the Supreme Court's apparent shift to the left is but a small part of the ways in which the government's place in civil society has shifted.

With the tremendous increase in responsibilities that the government has shouldered in recent decades, its influence can now be felt in virtually every corner of society. A farmer in Kansas who wishes to plant wheat finds himself subject to acreage restrictions and probably winds up selling some of his crop to the government under a federal price-support program. A community center in Colorado has to install wheelchair ramps and post exit signs in order to qualify for state funds under a federal grant-in-aid program. A small church in Connecticut votes to hire an accountant because IRS and Social Security regulations demand clearer, more accurate, audited financial reports. Little wonder, then, that churches have become more conscious of the state. Those who have decried the Supreme Court's decisions have also felt themselves encircled by laws and regulations unheard of in the past.

The newsletters and magazines of conservative religious organizations are filled with horror stories detailing the state's encroachment on their religious freedom. A teenager in New Jersey reported being reprimanded by school authorities for wearing a T-shirt bearing the name of a Christian rock group. A preacher in Florida warned followers that Federal Communications Commission (FCC) rulings were threatening to close his ministry. Three couples in North Dakota were said to have been convicted for not sending their children to public schools because of religious commitments. In view of incursions such as these, religious leaders have urged their parishioners to become more politically minded: awareness is the watchword, freedom the slogan, and action the mandate.

The irony of the situation is that the very Supreme Court cases church leaders have found vexing have often been initiated as protests against other kinds of government intrusion. Finding themselves at odds with local school boards, religious organizations have brought suits to gain equal time for the teaching of creation alongside evolution in the classroom. They have sought support from the courts for including more explicit lessons about religion in history courses and in social science courses. They have even supplied *amici curiae* briefs in cases involving Mormons, Jehovah's Witnesses, Moonies, and others with whom they are in fundamental theological disagreement. In all these ways, agencies of the state have been invited to play an ever more active role in determining the bounds of religion's involvement in the public sphere.

A word of caution is in order, though. The expanded role of government has not come about through the scheming of Washington bureaucrats who have hoodwinked an unwitting electorate into footing the bill. Such rhetoric has been the stuff of which successful presidential campaigns have been made. But it is rhetoric rather than reality.

Government has grown because of the public's interest in economic prosperity, its fear of economic and military insecurity, and its commitment to standards of fairness and equality. Particular regulations are always debated, but even the owner who thinks his ox is gored prefers a system of laws to a Hobbesian war of all against all.

Few object, for example, when the government steps in to find out why money contributed to a television preacher is being used as hush money for the preacher's mistress. Few object when government officials investigate the death of school children in an improperly maintained church-owned bus. And few object when criminal charges are brought against a true believer who firebombed birth control clinics because of religious convictions.

All of these are worthy causes—at least in most people's minds. Nevertheless, they increasingly draw government into areas in which the constitutionally guaranteed right to freedom of religion is potentially endangered. Thus, religious groups of all kinds have found themselves having to keep a more watchful eye on the public domain, and the mere fact of having to do so seems to color religious discourse with political hues. Gone is the village church protected by the benign consensus of a homogeneous town elite, the geographic isolation of the frontier, and the distance and ineffectiveness of a weak, decentralized government.

The present reality is more like that of Europe historically—in which religious convictions always had deep political overtones as well. Or at least this is the specter that some fear is haunting the United States. But this comparison is only partially accurate. It is accurate to the extent that government is now implicated in many of the regulations to which religious groups are subject and in many of the social issues about which religious groups are concerned. It is not accurate in that government in the United States is still prohibited from recognizing any one faith as an established religion, does not contribute directly to the financial support of religious institutions, and does not involve itself in the training and selection of clergy.

For all its growth, the impact of government on American religion in recent decades has been more indirect than direct. In those areas in which the hand of government has been nakedly active—such as the Supreme Court rulings on abortion and school prayer—religious groups have mobilized to let their wishes be known. Sometimes they have failed—and the very act of mobilizing may have kept them from focusing on more important matters. But they were able to voice their opinions, and if political action proved ineffective, to mount media campaigns aimed at modifying public opinion, or to sponsor private initiatives (such as pregnancy clinics and Christian schools) as end runs around government policies. In many areas, though, the hand of government has remained hidden; that is, policies and programs with seemingly little relevance to religion have been advanced, and yet the social impact of these policies and programs on religion has turned out to be extremely significant. These are the areas in which greater understanding has been especially needed because both the state and religious groups themselves have not been as cognizant of their effects.

A New Class

This brings me to a final argument that bears directly on the recent controversies over the role of religion in public affairs. It has been suggested that these controversies have deepened because of a change in the class structure of American society. For example, sociologist Peter Berger has written of the rise to prominence of a new class of people "who make their living from the production and distribution of symbolic knowledge." It is this class, he argues, that has enlivened the strength of liberals, radicals, and secular humanists, on the one hand, and prompted the conservative Protestant upsurge as a reaction, on the other hand. Berger links a number of issues concerning the relations between church and state to this basic *klassenkamp*, as he calls it: abortion, feminism, military policy, even environmental questions.[30]

30. Peter L. Berger, "American Religion: Conservative Upsurge, Liberal Prospects," in *Liberal Protestantism: Realities and Possibilities*, ed. Robert S. Michaelsen and

This argument is useful, as far as it goes, particularly because it highlights the conflict that has emerged within American religion. Conservative groups are not the only ones that have been paying increasing attention to the role of religion in public affairs. Liberal groups have also been active, often taking positions directly opposed to those advocated by conservatives. But the idea of a new class needs to be amended in at least three important respects.

First, we need to see it in connection with what I have already said about the effects of state expansion. The new class is not the product of some inevitable cultural force promoting the expansion of symbol production: the media, schools, higher education, and so on. It may be associated with the economic development that some have described as a transition from industrial to postindustrial capitalism. But it is also the product of specific initiatives by the state. It has come about because of government initiatives such as the G.I. Bill after World War II to promote higher education, the decision in the late 1950s to explore outer space after the Russians' launching of Sputnik, and the federal government's commitment to enormous expenditures for higher education during the 1960s. If a new class has arisen that has fundamentally altered the religious views of those within it and prompted a conservative reaction from those outside it, then the government's hand in this development must be recognized. This has been one of the significant ways in which government policy has had indirect consequences for American religion.

Second, we need to recognize that the argument about a new class suggests something other than a simple hierarchical image of class distinctions. Those who constitute the new class may be privileged with respect to educational levels and jobs in professional occupations. But the new class also represents a new way of measuring class position. It reflects distinctions in the capacity to use knowledge, whereas older measures of class reflected differences in material wealth. Thus, members of the new class may not be as privileged as some members of other classes in terms of income, possessions, inherited wealth, and so on. This means that members of the new class do not always simply get their way because they have more resources than everyone else. Members of other classes still command resources, too. So when

---

Wade Clark Roof (New York: Pilgrim Press, 1986), pp. 19-36 (see especially pp. 25-28). For other connections between evangelicalism and the new class, see James Davison Hunter, *Evangelicalism: The Coming Generation* (Chicago: University of Chicago Press, 1987).

it comes to religious disputes, both sides may be able to call on influential elites to give them backing.

Finally, the idea of a new class needs to be amended to clarify
the role that cultural capital (or cultural resources, if one prefers a less
Marxist-sounding phrase) plays in religious disputes. The cultural capital of the new class has generally been recognized: knowledge gained
from higher education, cosmopolitanism, verbal communication skills.
Those opposed to the new class, though, have their own forms of cultural capital. They are likely to have command of their religious heritage—hence the value they attach to biblical inerrancy. They participate in the wider fruits of a technological society—witness the use of
cable television hookups by television preachers. They have successfully participated in the general growth of higher education by spon-
soring their own colleges. And, while underrepresented in many social scientific and humanistic disciplines, they are likely to have gained
leaders with training in technical subjects such as business administration, engineering, and computer science.

If the conservative upsurge is indeed a backlash against the
rise of a new class, as Peter Berger suggests, it is a rebellion with significant resources at its disposal. Consequently, it is difficult to picture
the present controversies over the proper role of faith in public affairs
simply as a transition to a more enlightened, secular, or postmodern
situation. It seems more accurate to say that societal changes have nurtured both the new class and its opposition. To the extent that each
has different views on a wide range of issues, including theological
and moral orientations, then it appears likely that the role of religion
in public affairs will continue to be hotly contested.

PROSPECTS AND IMPLICATIONS

What are the implications? For specific issues, the tug-of-war currently evident between religious conservatives and religious liberals is likely to be determined more by events within the political arena than by
efforts on the part of religious groups alone. This is not to say that
those efforts are unimportant: in view of the relative balance that seems
to exist between conservatives and liberals on many issues, active and
well-organized efforts are always consequential. This same balance,
however, means that other factors—factors over which religious
groups have only partial control—may be even more consequential.
For example, the fallout from the sex scandals involving television

preachers Jim Bakker and Jimmy Swaggart in 1987 could prove significant enough that political candidates in the future will downplay their affinities with evangelicalism entirely. If so, religious conservatives may have more difficulty in the future making claims on these candidates. Or, to take another example, the eruption of a major war in Central America in which troops from the United States were involved could radically shift public opinion, one way or the other, no matter how vigorously various religious factions supported or opposed strong defensive postures.

The most that can be predicted on specific issues is that these issues will continue to be subjects of intense debate by religious groups. Having mobilized to achieve a ban on abortions, religious conservatives seem unlikely to demobilize again should their goal be attained. Nor do religious liberals seem likely to abandon the field should a Supreme Court decision on abortion turn against them. Each side is too well organized, has too many programs that are dependent on arousing concern about contemporary issues, and has become too aware of the importance of public affairs to retreat entirely into isolated self-contemplation.

A second area in which the implications of the present controversies need to be recognized concerns the broader tensions that have been produced within American religion itself. At one time, the deepest tensions dividing the faithful from one another consisted of hostilities between Protestants and Catholics and between Christians and Jews. At the present juncture, these tensions pale beside the ones that have arisen between religious conservatives and religious liberals.

Not content to differ merely on specific issues, such as abortion or school prayer, religious activists have turned to denouncing the very premises of their opponents' religious convictions. On the conservative side, fundamentalists and evangelicals express doubts that their liberal brethren can still be counted as Christians at all. For example, in a direct-mail solicitation from the conservative Christian Action Council, executive director Curtis J. Young observed that abortions were being performed in a number of hospitals that had been founded by mainline Protestant denominations. Shocked at this outrage, he went on to castigate these institutions for rejecting Christ and keeping only the name of a faith that had "long since been abandoned." In his view it was an "outrage against God" for these hospitals to retain any identity at all with Christianity.[31]   *more polarized !*

31. Quoted from a letter dated July 1987.

Some hospital administrators might agree. Or we might conclude simply that this is the hyperbole of which direct-mail solicitations are necessarily composed. But the same kind of invective creeps into the pew as well. To wit: two parishioners were overheard discussing a recent study suggesting that students at evangelical colleges were no longer being indoctrinated effectively into orthodox statements of belief. Said one: "Perhaps it is good they are learning to think for themselves." Replied the other: "Well, I shouldn't have even raised it with you; I can see you're moving away from Christianity entirely."

Nor is this merely the closed-mindedness of fundamentalists. Religious liberals have been equally closed-minded in denouncing fundamentalists. "Not Buddhism, not Hinduism, not Islam, but fundamentalism—it is the one thing that is anathema to the gospel," one clergyman declared from the pulpit. Judging from the increasingly negative attitudes toward evangelicals and fundamentalists expressed in public opinion polls, pronouncements such as these are probably not uncommon.

There is, of course, a long history of ill will in the United States between religious conservatives and liberals. But the recent controversies appear to have deepened these sentiments. Each side has become more visible to the other. The rhetoric of direct-mail solicitations has become more strident and the editorial commentary of the media more shrill. To the highly nuanced theological discussions that have been familiar in the past—and that have often been confined within denominational boundaries—have been added the politicized "I win—you lose" stakes of public confrontation. The end result has been a travesty of the profession of love, forgiveness, and mutual forbearance.

Mention also needs to be made of the significance of the present controversies for our broader conceptions of ourselves as citizens and as morally responsible individuals. From one perspective, controversies over the appropriate relations between church and state may be regarded as troublesome issues to be gotten through as quickly as possible. Not the process but the final result is all that matters. Nevertheless, from another perspective it behooves us to recognize that the process is also important.

Uncertainties in the relations between church and state provide occasions for moral pedagogy. We are forced on these occasions to discuss our basic values—our conceptions of what it means to be virtuous, upright, responsible citizens. If we pay close attention to the flood of words that flows from any church-state debate, we discover that these words go well beyond the practical, the technical, the legal.

They remind us of the moral timber of which a strong nation is constructed. They tell us again that the free expression of faith is indeed a sacred right. They speak of the cherished past and an endangered future. They picture the state in its role as guardian of decency and democracy. They commend citizenship and enhance awareness of the public sphere. This moral pedagogy, even more so than the specific issues under consideration, is perhaps the greatest function performed by the ongoing debate over faith and public affairs.

What, then, must we conclude about the role of faith in shaping America's democratic public philosophy, given the social and cultural contexts in which public debate now takes place? Do we stand on a precipice and gaze into a netherworld of diminishing democratic ideals—a future fraught more and more with totalitarian threats and narrowly utilitarian struggles? Or does our tradition remain strong, perhaps even in a way that promises greater creative energy for American democracy in the future?

Now, as always in the past, the answer lies somewhere between these extremes. Both the realities of the present world and the eschatological images embedded deep within the Judeo-Christian tradition call us to be mindful of the dangers that lie along each side of our path and the opportunities that call us to move forward.

The dangers are clear, even if they need to be pointed out again and again in order to keep us vigilant. They arise both from the scourge of totalitarian regimes to which religious conservatives have given so much attention and from the mindless greed of a global economic system that values nothing so highly as profits and market expansion—the greed that generates many of the social injustices to which religious liberals have called our attention.

They also arise from our own manner of dealing with the social and economic contingencies that beset us. A democratic government that steadily expands its bureaucratic functions in order to promote economic growth—especially one that legitimates its own growth in antibureaucratic, laissez faire rhetoric—is most to be feared as a travesty of democracy itself. Sadly, thus far we have paid far too little attention to the implications of such growth for the shaping of our public philosophy.

At minimum, discussions of public philosophy must pay heed to the increasing role of government to shape religion directly—and, indeed, to shape the society directly—through tax policies, the funding of research, entitlement programs, fiscal transfer policies, the location and maintenance of a vast military, and so on. Public philosophy may take form most explicitly in debates generated by the courts. But our lives may be shaped even more decidedly by policies and practices that never become matters of conscious public debate. When this happens, the danger is one of having our national destiny decided for us *tout court*, rather than having stumbled into an improper mix of religious and secular values.

The danger besetting us also lies to a great extent in the bifurcation that has taken place in American religion between religious liberals and religious conservatives. As long as this division remains uppermost, we can perhaps take comfort that at least two sides to every issue will be presented. But we must ask whether two sides are sufficient, or whether five or six—or a hundred—would not be more in the interest of maintaining a creative public philosophy.

We also must ask whether the task of presenting arguments and counterarguments in the public sphere—at congressional hearings, in court, on television talk shows, and even at academic conferences—is always beneficial to the primary work for which religious bodies exist. The danger in promoting public philosophy through a hearty application of religious principles may be that we gain the world but lose the soul on which those very principles have always rested.

The positive side—the opportunities that lie before us—can perhaps be summarized more succinctly. Our religious debates still inform the public arena in important ways. They lead us along paths of tolerance and forbearance (if only by negative example at times). They continue to undergird many of our specific concerns about public morality, compassion, and social justice. Perhaps more indirectly, they infuse public philosophy with broad conceptions of equality, virtue, and civic responsibility, and they clothe these conceptions with the rich biblical narratives that render them intelligible and give them rhetorical power. Therefore, a time of ferment in public religion is likely to draw larger segments of the population into the cause of democracy and to instruct them in the practical principles on which democracy is founded.

Beset on the one hand with the grave dangers to which many social analysts have alerted us, and faced on the other hand with great opportunities to revitalize and enrich our public philosophy, we must proceed with both caution and diligence. Careful scrutiny of the new conditions that characterize our society and our world must be added to the chorus of recollections about our past that continuously seek to find new meanings and insights in the constitutional heritage and cultural wisdom of years gone by. In the task of settling immediate problems, we must be reminded of the value of the broader questions that these problems raise. Perhaps above all, we must sensitize ourselves increasingly to the ways in which our implicit assumptions govern even the ways in which we pose the enduring questions about our public philosophy.

Four

Struggle in
One Denomination

PRESBYTERIANS AS A TYPICAL CASE

THE TITLE OF THIS CHAPTER—"Struggle in One Denomination"—is, I
am afraid, somewhat reminiscent of the title of one of Stalin's best-
known articles: "Socialism in One Country."[1] I do not wish to conjure
up any impertinent comparisons between the Soviet Union and
American Presbyterianism. But the similarity in phrasing is not entirely coincidental.

In 1924 Stalin's Russia was beleaguered on every side. It was
not the only country in which socialism was being advanced. It had,
however, risen to the forefront of the international socialist movement,
at least for a brief time, only to find itself caught up in a world far more
complex than its theoreticians had predicted.

Presbyterianism in the United States has from the beginning
been one of our flagship denominational traditions. It is now faced
with a world far different and more complex than any world it has
faced before. The turmoil it has experienced within its ranks during
the past several decades is by no means unique. Indeed, this turmoil
can be found in nearly all the major American denominations and
faiths. And yet, it is hard to find another denomination in which the

---

1. Stalin's article was published in *Pravda* on December 20, 1924.

turmoil has been as notable in its magnitude or as profound in its consequences.

In the previous chapters I attempted to outline some of the broad contours of this turmoil in the nation at large.[2] Starting with the years immediately after World War II, I discussed the institutional and cultural climate of American religion in the 1940s and 1950s, showing some of the preconditions that were to reinforce later conflicts, and then traced the trajectory of these conflicts into the 1980s and suggested some of their cultural and political implications. Here, I would like to consider the ways in which Presbyterianism reflects these broader patterns, how it may depart from them, and what the turmoil it presently faces may suggest for its clergy and members in the immediate future. As I shall suggest shortly, the Presbyterian case has much to teach all of us about the dilemmas of faith in American society at the end of the twentieth century.

In one sense, of course, Presbyterians are not a typical case. To a greater extent than many other denominations, they have suffered a long history of conflict between theologically liberal and theologically conservative factions, and for this reason the current cleavage between liberals and conservatives that we shall be considering may represent less of a restructuring for them than it does for American religion more generally.

The conflicts and schisms that have characterized Presbyterian history have been documented by students of American religion. No sooner had the first General Presbytery been founded in Philadelphia in 1706 than tensions began to erupt. Conservatives, largely consisting of recent Scottish and Scotch-Irish immigrants to Pennsylvania, argued that membership and church discipline be contingent on strict adherence to the Westminster Confession; liberals, who tended to be concentrated more in the New York and New England presbyteries, argued that the Bible alone was a sufficient rule of faith and practice.

After several attempts at compromise and reconciliation in the 1720s, the conflict grew more intense with the advent of revivalism and an emphasis on personal conversion that developed during the Great Awakening. The more liberal "New Side," as it was called, preached revivalism and an experiential knowledge of Christ, while the "Old Side" stood for a more corporatist form of church discipline rooted in the Westminster tradition. Each side claimed authority in

---

2. See also Robert Wuthnow, *The Restructuring of American Religion: Society and Faith Since World War II* (Princeton: Princeton University Press, 1988).

matters of doctrine and clergy training, and both sides institutionalized their claims in concrete organizations, most notable of which was
the New Side's founding of the College of New Jersey at Princeton
in 1746.

Conflict between "Old School" and "New School" Presbyterians erupted again with considerable intensity during the first
decades of the nineteenth century. Revivalism and the Reformed tradition in doctrine and church government, control of mission boards,
and cooperation with other denominations in ventures such as the
founding of Union Theological Seminary in 1836 served as foci of contention. The two factions officially split from one another in 1837 and
remained divided until 1869. Meanwhile, other schisms were also
dividing Presbyterians into a more diverse range of denominations,
including the Cumberland Presbyterian Church (founded in 1810), the
1833 split between the Reformed Presbyterian Church General Synod
and the Reformed Presbyterian Church of North America, and the formation of the Presbyterian Church U.S. in the South in 1861 at the
outset of the Civil War.[3]

In the twentieth century, Presbyterians' involvement in the
conflict between fundamentalists and modernists again sets their history apart from that of many other denominations. The conflict was
particularly intense among Presbyterians because it revolved around a
number of hotly contested issues: what missionaries had to do to
receive denominational support, views of the Bible, doctrines about
the Virgin Birth and the Second Coming of Christ, different perspectives on the historic role of Calvinism, and conflict between premil-
lennialists and postmillennialists. Official splits resulting from the controversy between fundamentalists and liberals included the founding
of the Orthodox Presbyterian Church in 1936 and the Bible Presbyterian Church in 1937. Only among Northern Baptists were the battles waged by the fundamentalists as intense.

The Presbyterians' legacy of conflict, however, needs to be understood in perspective. Despite the denomination's early cleavages in
the nineteenth century and its involvement in the fundamentalist-
modernist controversy, it has not been any more prone to schisms in
the twentieth century than the other large denominational families. At
least this is the tentative conclusion that has emerged thus far from re-

3. I have drawn this summary primarily from Sydney E. Ahlstrom, *A Religious
History of the American People* (New Haven: Yale University Press, 1972), pp. 267-79, 462-
71.

search on schisms that I have done with several of my colleagues. We have analyzed data on 175 denominations, including 55 Baptist denominations, 50 Lutheran denominations, 34 Methodist denominations, and 36 Presbyterian and Reformed denominations, between 1890 and 1980. Among these denominations, there were 55 schisms.

Presbyterians actually had somewhat *higher* probabilities of survival (i.e., *lower* probabilities of schism) than did Methodists, Baptists, or Lutherans, though the differences were not statistically significant. We also performed two other tests that bear on the question of whether Presbyterians have been more prone to schisms over the past century than other denominational families. We took account of other factors to see if denominational family still made any difference in the likelihood of schisms occurring. When we did so, denominational family produced no significant effects. We also examined the effects of church polity type, a variable we coded separately to be able to compare the rate of schisms among denominations with congregational, presbyterian, or episcopal forms of church government. Again, we found no significant differences.[4]

In one sense, however, the Presbyterian family provides an unusually good opportunity for examining the growing cleavage between religious liberals and religious conservatives and other tensions that have surfaced in American religion in recent years. For some years, the denomination has been in the forefront of efforts by denominational agencies themselves to collect systematic data on the beliefs and attitudes of its laity and clergy. Large numbers of questions have been asked over the past decade and a half to random samples of laity and clergy included in the "Presbyterian Panel." Several books and numerous articles have been published from these data. In addition, it is possible to flesh out the nature of changes among Presbyterians through their many denominational reports, annual minutes, and monthly publications.

4. These conclusions are from Robert C. Liebman, John R. Sutton, and Robert Wuthnow, "Exploring the Social Sources of Denominationalism: Schisms in American Protestant Denominations, 1890-1980," *American Sociological Review* 53 (1988): 343-52. Some additional findings are given in John R. Sutton, Robert Wuthnow, and Robert C. Liebman, "Organizational Foundings: Schisms in American Protestant Denominations, 1890-1980," presented at the 1988 meeting of the American Sociological Association in Atlanta, Georgia. Copies of these and subsequent papers can be obtained from John R. Sutton, Department of Sociology, University of California, Santa Barbara, California.

THE DECLINING SIGNIFICANCE OF PRESBYTERIANISM

The first conclusion that emerges clearly from all this evidence is that Presbyterianism has experienced a serious decline during the past three decades. Of course, denominational officials have commented extensively on the decline in membership. Since 1966, the Presbyterian Church, U.S.A., has declined by more than 1.2 million members—a decrease of approximately 30 percent. Church school membership and infant baptisms—the most reliable predictors of vitality in the future—have declined even more precipitously: by 52 percent and 35 percent, respectively. Over the past two decades, the typical Presbyterian congregation has seen its members slip from an average of 326 to an average of 256. Despite many new churches, the denomination has suffered a net loss of more than 1,400 congregations.[5] These losses suggest a serious decline in the denomination itself.

Moreover, the *perception* of decline has become truly widespread among Presbyterians. Not only has it become a recurrent theme in deliberations at the General Assembly, but it has also become a widely recognized phenomenon in local congregations. Thus, according to one study, only one member in eight thought his or her congregation was growing faster than its surrounding community, while one member in two thought his or her congregation was either growing more slowly or declining faster than the community.[6]

But another kind of decline may be even more indicative of the changes facing established religious bodies in our society—the decline of *denominationalism.* By all indications, Presbyterians have not only been diminishing in numbers but have also experienced an erosion in the social and cultural boundaries that have historically set them off from other denominations as a distinctive religious entity. This erosion will come as no surprise to many within the denomination (or in other mainline Protestant denominations), but it may still be instructive to understand more specifically the ways in which it has happened.

First, some of the social characteristics that used to set Presbyterians off from the rest of the American population have diminished at least marginally in importance. For example, in 1960 Pres-

---

5. Figures are for 1987, the most recent year available, and 1966 (United Presbyterian Church and Presbyterian Church, U.S., combined), the year when the United Presbyterian Church membership losses began; reported in *The Presbyterian Layman,* July/August 1988, p. 5.

6. *Presbyterian Panel,* September 1986, p. A16.

byterians were 1.8 times more likely than average to be employed in professional or managerial occupations, but by 1976 they were only 1.4 times more likely to be employed in these occupations.[7] Similarly, in 1956 Presbyterians had been 1.9 times as likely to have attained some college education than was true in the nation as a whole. By 1980, this factor had been reduced to 1.6 times the national average.[8] Over the same period, even more dramatic changes took place in the social characteristics of other denominations. Consequently, Roman Catholics, Baptists, Lutherans, and even members of fundamentalist sects in the 1980s all resembled Presbyterians more closely on basic social characteristics than they did in the 1950s or 1960s.

Perhaps because of these convergences, Presbyterians as a group also do not differ markedly from the members of other denominations on some of the most salient social and political issues of our time. For instance, attitudes toward abortion have been particularly divisive in the political arena since the Supreme Court's ruling in *Roe* v. *Wade* in 1973; and yet, on a standard survey question during this period that asked persons whether they approved of abortion for someone who simply did not want more children, the percentages answering yes ranged only between 44 percent among Lutherans, Catholics, and members of Protestant sects, and 50 percent among Episcopalians. Baptists, Methodists, Presbyterians, and Jews all scored about midway between these two figures.[9]

Second, much evidence suggests that more Presbyterians mingle with, marry the members of, and switch to other denominations now than ever before. For example, data collected in the 1970s and early 1980s showed that 45 percent of all Americans who had been raised as Presbyterians now belonged to some other denomina-

---

7. These data were calculated from the 1960 and 1976 National Election Surveys, conducted by the Center for Political Studies at the University of Michigan. Major surveys are conducted every four years during presidential elections; minor surveys are conducted midway between the major studies during congressional elections. The data analyzed were on tapes at the Princeton University Computer Center made available through the Inter-University Consortium for Political and Social Research at the University of Michigan.

8. The 1956 data are from the national survey conducted by the Census Bureau in that year, as reported in Bernard Lazerwitz, "Religion and Social Structure in the United States," in *Religion, Culture and Society: A Reader in the Sociology of Religion*, ed. Louis Schneider (New York: Wiley, 1964), pp. 426-39. The 1980 figures were derived from the National Election Survey data from that year.

9. From my analysis of the General Social Survey Cumulative Data File for the years 1972-1982.

tion or to no denomination at all,[10] Interdenominational marriages also point to a weakening of denominational boundaries. Specifically, a comparison of data from the mid-1970s and the mid-1950s shows that the percentage of married people with spouses belonging to the same religion as themselves declined by 25 percentage points among Presbyterians over this period.[11]

Third, all of this takes place within a more general climate of theological and cultural tolerance. In the 1940s and 1950s, deep misgivings still separated the members of many Protestant denominations and, particularly, Protestants from Roman Catholics. For example, in an article warning Protestant youth against marrying Catholics, a Presbyterian pastor wrote: "It is Protestant theology, not Roman Catholic, which has provoked men to demand free government and the overthrow of tyrants. . . . It is Protestant church polity, and not Roman Catholic, which schools men in the actual practice of democracy."[12] A few years later the Presbyterian Church, U.S.A., adopted a statement at its annual convention that condemned the "cultic worship of Mary" among Catholics. Since the Second Vatican Council, such expressions of anti-Catholicism by Presbyterian leaders have, to say the least, become unfashionable and for the most part unspeakable.

In the years immediately after World War II, greater cooperation between Presbyterians and other Protestant denominations was often hard to promote. A 1946 effort by Episcopalians and Presbyterians to encourage merger negotiations ran aground from stubborn resistance rooted in historical and liturgical differences. Even among Presbyterians themselves, little headway toward greater cooperation was made in these years. At the same time the Episcopal-Presbyterian negotiations were foundering; for example, an effort by the northern and southern wings of Presbyterianism to achieve doctrinal unity was firmly defeated.

Clear evidence on grass-roots tolerance of other denominations is more difficult to find, but some evidence suggests that laity may have been more willing to transcend denominational boundaries

10. These data are also from an analysis of the General Social Survey Cumulative Data File, 1972-1982. They are based on nearly 12,000 cases from representative adult samples of the U.S. population.

11. The data for the 1950s are reported in Andrew M. Greeley, *The Denominational Society: A Sociological Approach to Religion in America* (Glenview, IL: Scott, Foresman, 1972), p. 245. The data for the 1970s are from an analysis of the General Social Survey Cumulative File, 1972-1982.

12. See Ware W. Wimberly, "The Mixed Marriage," *Presbyterian Tribune,* January 1946, pp. 9-10.

for a longer period of time than these actions by clergy and denominational officials would imply. For instance, a representative survey of more than seven thousand respondents from seventeen denominations in 1932 found majority support, despite some personal misgivings about the beliefs and practices of other denominations, for some kind of church union or cooperation in all but three denominations. Methodists and Presbyterians were opposed to maintaining present denominational divisions by a ratio of four to one, Northern Baptists and Episcopalians were marginally against maintaining the present order, while Lutherans, Southern Presbyterians, and Southern Baptists leaned moderately toward continuing the current divisions. Moreover, those who favored greater interdenominational cooperation were about as likely to favor uniting the various bodies into a single church as they were to support the idea of merely creating a federation of denominations.[13]

With social differences among denominations eroding, intermarriage across denominational lines increasing, and tolerance levels in the culture more generally rising, any particularistic tendencies separating the members of mainline Protestant denominations appear to have become limited to the marginal few. Thus when sociologists Charles Glock and Rodney Stark surveyed church members in California in the early 1960s, fewer than one Presbyterian in ten thought membership in a particular faith was necessary for salvation.[14] In the late 1970s, a national study of Lutherans showed that four in five were interested in having cooperative worship services with Presbyterians and that three in four favored common services with Baptists and Catholics.[15]

Finally, the erosion of denominational barriers has been legitimated by theological and ecclesiastical pronouncements by the denomination itself. The ecumenical movement has played an important role in fostering greater cooperation between Presbyterians and other denominations. One of the most auspicious features of this movement was the founding of the Consultation on Church Union, brought into being

13. See "The Sentiment for Church Union," in *Yearbook of American Churches: 1933*, ed. Herman C. Weber (New York: Roundtable Press, 1933), pp. 308-11.

14. Charles Y. Glock and Rodney Stark, *Christian Beliefs and Anti-Semitism* (New York: Harper & Row, 1966), p. 23.

15. I conducted this survey in 1979 as part of the "Lutheran Listening Post," a national survey of the members of the Lutheran Church in America. Some results from this survey have been reported in Roger A. Johnson, ed., *Views from the Pews* (Philadelphia: Fortress Press, 1983).

in 1962 by the United Presbyterian Church, U.S.A., the Episcopal Church, the Methodist Church, and the United Church of Christ to explore possibilities for greater cooperation and eventual union among these denominations. And the northern and southern branches of Presbyterianism finally came together again in 1983.

The denomination has also enacted legislation specifically aimed at lowering denominational barriers and making it easier for clergy and laity alike to cross these boundaries. The 1967 Confession denied that belief in any particular confession could be held as a standard of membership or a criteria of belief. It has also become easier for clergy trained in seminaries outside the denomination to be ordained. For example, an estimated half of all Presbyterian clergy no longer receive training in the denomination's seminaries.

SOCIAL FORCES AND THE DENOMINATION'S RESPONSE

Like other denominational families, Presbyterianism has been exposed on every side to the serious changes taking place in American society since World War II. In the 1950s, its members grew as the population itself grew. Young families moved to the suburbs, earned good salaries, and took their children to church. Much of the fundamentalism that had dogged the denomination's flanks in the 1930s was now isolated in the smaller Presbyterian sects, and neo-orthodoxy was heard loudly in the denomination's major seminaries. Church leaders called for a moderate blend of personal salvation, evangelism, missionary effort, and social outreach.

In the 1960s, Presbyterians soon became caught up in the larger turmoil of the society. Formal resolutions against racial discrimination gradually gave way to more activist involvement in the civil rights movement. Crises in the cities became the subject of commission reports. By the end of the decade, campus protests, black militance, and the Vietnam War were all matters to which church leaders were giving serious attention.

Studies of Presbyterians and other mainstream Protestant denominations in the 1960s and early 1970s suggested that the clergy had moved to the left, which meant championing social justice and minority causes, far more rapidly than the typical parishioner. However, a substantial shift was taking place among laity during this period as well—a shift that gave left-leaning clergy more grass-roots support as time went on. This was the shift associated with the rapid upgrading in educational levels that the federal government began to sponsor in the 1960s.

Unless one was an Episcopalian, attending college had been rare among the members of all denominations in the 1950s. Fewer than one Baptist, Lutheran, or Catholic in seven had ever been to college; and even among Presbyterians the proportion was only one in three. By the early 1980s, six Presbyterians in ten had been to college.

This change had a number of important consequences. As young people went through the nation's colleges in the 1960s and 1970s, many swelled the ranks of Presbyterian campus ministries, often providing foot soldiers for the social and political activities of these ministries. Other young people left the church, finding it too staid and traditional, especially in comparison with the dynamism of political movements, communes, and new religious imports from East Asia. The geographic and social mobility and greater levels of tolerance associated with higher education increased the likelihood that young Presbyterians would marry outside their own faith, move away from parent congregations, and leave the denomination entirely. The quest for higher education forced young people to postpone marriage and childrearing, resulting in some of the numeric decline the denomination has experienced. And the division between those with better educations and those with lower levels of formal training began to reinforce differences between Presbyterians with liberal theological inclinations and Presbyterians with more conservative and evangelical orientations.

Other social changes influenced the organizational structure of American Presbyterianism directly. As I mentioned earlier, our studies of schisms and mergers show no differences between Presbyterians and other denominational families in their propensity to have undergone these organizational changes, at least in the twentieth century. Our research does, however, reveal the extent to which Presbyterians and the other denominational families alike have been subject to the effects of broader strains in their environment. We found that an increase in size, such as the growth that occurred in the 1950s, was an important predictor of subsequent schisms. This is not to say that strife develops more easily in good times than in bad. But it does suggest that larger memberships become increasingly difficult to control, other things being equal.

Instability in the broader economic environment, especially business failures—a phenomenon that became increasingly evident in the 1960s and 1970s—proved to be associated with higher rates of denominational schisms. We also found that prior mergers, of the kind that many major denominations entered into during the 1960s and 1970s, increase the likelihood of schisms occurring. And we found a kind of contagion effect among schisms themselves: a few schisms in the broader environment seem to diminish the likelihood of other schisms occurring, but large numbers of schisms greatly increase the likelihood of other schisms. This pattern was especially prominent in the 1960s and early 1970s. We also know from examining the accounts of these schisms that theological cleavages were generally an important factor.

THE STRUGGLE BETWEEN LIBERALS AND CONSERVATIVES

As denominational boundaries have generally diminished in influence, a new division has risen in importance. At the national level, much evidence suggests that this division, as we have seen in previous chapters, can best be characterized simply as a division between self-styled religious liberals and religious conservatives. According to national studies, the population divides itself almost evenly between these two categories, with various gradations of extremity and moderation in each. Each of the major religious groupings for which large enough numbers can be obtained also seems to reflect this division. Lutherans, Baptists, Methodists, and Roman Catholics all have about equal numbers of religious liberals and religious conservatives among their members. Evidence also suggests considerable animosity and misgiving on the part of each faction toward the other. Perhaps correctly, religious liberals view their evangelical counterparts as narrow-minded dogmatists, and evangelicals suspect religious liberals of having become doctrinally and morally permissive, if not outrightly secular.

Some time ago, a book by sociologist of religion Dean Hoge, fittingly titled *Division in the Protestant House,* pointed to the presence of a cleavage of much the same kind among Presbyterians. Based on data from Presbyterian clergy and laity in the early 1970s, Hoge's research showed that those who emphasized personal evangelism were deeply divided from those who emphasized social action. Not only did the two factions have widely differing views of what the church should be doing, but they differed fundamentally from one another on theological issues and in social backgrounds as well. Although there was among clergy at least a neo-orthodox group who occupied middle ground, theological liberals constituted a clearly identified group at one end of the spectrum, and theological conservatives constituted another self-identified group at the other end of the spectrum, and the two groups assigned very different priorities to the various activities and ministries of the church.[16]

In more recent years, harsh words of the kind one might expect to hear Democrats and Republicans leveling at one another have fanned the flames of tension between Presbyterian liberals and Presbyterian conservatives. At the 1988 meeting of the General Assembly, for example, an elder from the Pittsburgh Presbytery succeeded in getting disciplinary action taken against the conservative Presbyterian Lay Committee by charging it with invading the privacy of her congregation's members. The Committee, she alleged, was led by "unscrupulous people," whose access to church membership lists could "enable them to defraud, harass or even terrorize the people in a congregation."[17] Equally harsh words about Presbyterian liberals can be found routinely in conservative publications like *The Presbyterian Layman.*

Studies conducted by the denomination itself show the extent to which Presbyterians are currently divided over a number of issues that have become salient as matters of church policy. One study showed that about four members in ten believe the denomination should work to pressure the government of South Africa to end apartheid, while about three in ten were opposed to this kind of activity.[18] Gender, feminism, and the ordination of women is another topic that has produced much division of opinion. Ordination has apparently begun to evoke fairly widespread consensus, although half of all members still fear that appointing a woman in their own congregation would create strife.[19] But the roles of women more generally remain matters over which Presbyterians are divided. One study found that three members in ten thought "women should worry less about their rights and more about becoming good wives and mothers," while four in ten disagreed.[20]

As in most other denominations and faith traditions, abortion has been a particularly divisive issue. According to national surveys, Presbyterians divide almost evenly between opponents of abortion and those who feel abortion should be a matter of individual choice. While

16. Dean R. Hoge, *Division in the Protestant House* (Philadelphia: Westminster Press, 1976).

17. *Presbyterian Layman,* July/August 1988, pp. 1, 4.

18. *Presbyterian Panel,* March 1987, p. A9.

19. *Presbyterian Panel,* September 1986, p. A3.

20. *Presbyterian Panel,* September 1987, p. A9.

results depend on how the question is asked, the proportions who express tolerant views toward abortion range from 47 percent to 56 percent.[21] Not only are Presbyterians divided in their views, but each side has also mobilized itself to press its views at governing meetings of the denomination and to the membership at large. For example, Presbyterians Pro-Life has pressed its ideas actively at both the congregational and national levels, most recently drawing a large crowd at the 1988 General Assembly to hear an impassioned plea for the unborn by its invited speaker, Mother Teresa of Calcutta.

From national surveys, one can also piece together evidence that shows the extent to which Presbyterians are divided on political orientations. For example, the ratio of self-identified political liberals to self-identified political conservatives is almost at parity: about one-third of all Presbyterians polled between the mid-1970s and early 1980s identified themselves as conservatives, about one-third identified themselves as liberals, and the remaining third took a middle-of-the-road position.[22]

These divisions in attitudes and theological identification have been reinforced by a new kind of organization within the denomination: the special purpose group. Although some of these groups—missionary societies, youth organizations, women's groups—have a long history among Presbyterians, their overall numbers have increased noticeably since the 1960s, and their character has changed as well. In fact, their impetus appears to have been closely linked with the more general turmoil in American society during the 1960s.

In anticipation of the confessional revision in 1967, leaders opposed to this revision formed two special purpose groups, and these movements soon gained national followings. One was the Presbyterian Lay Committee, which also played a prominent role in opposing the denomination's protest activities during the Vietnam War; the other was called Presbyterians United for Biblical Concerns. Both disseminated literature, organized petition campaigns, and lobbied at meetings of the denomination's General Assembly to uphold conservative views of the Bible, as well as to defend doctrines rooted in the Reformation tradition and strict concepts of moral and spiritual discipline.

Other special purpose groups include Presbyterians for Democracy and Religious Freedom, Presbyterians Pro-Life, Presbyterians

21. Based on an analysis of 383 Presbyterians polled in General Social Surveys between 1972 and 1982.
22. Data on this question were available from 250 Presbyterians polled in the General Social Survey between 1972 and 1984.

for Lesbian and Gay Concerns, the Witherspoon Society, the Black Presbyterian Caucus, Presbyterians for Biblical Sexuality, and the Religious Coalition on Abortion Rights. Like political action committees and lobbyist organizations in Washington, these special purpose groups have arisen within the denomination to mobilize grass-roots support for particular issues and make this support heard in the denomination's policy-making circles. They function within guidelines established by the denomination. But they clearly add a new layer of organization to the more established hierarchy of authority that has traditionally risen from the ranks of local elders and pastors through regional presbyteries and synods to the General Assembly.

Moreover, special purpose groups are not simply the work of like-minded individuals who wish to band together for more intimate fellowship or a stronger sense of community. They vary in purpose, and some do have community as their chief objective. But the majority resemble what sociologists have called "struggle groups": special interests organized specifically to engage in combat with other special interests, to champion their cause, and to see their cause win over the hearts and minds of denominational officials. In the words of a recent editorial in the newspaper of one such pressure group, "the church will be changed by a proliferation of sharply focused, single-issue groups, each of which is willing to get down in the trenches and fight."[23]

Despite the fact that these pressure groups are devoted to single issues, there has also been a notable tendency for them to stack up into two opposing camps, one championing conservative issues of all kinds, the other adopting liberal positions across the board. Thus, a group like the Presbyterian Lay Committee not only struggles to "put greater emphasis on the teaching of the Bible as the authoritative Word of God," as its official objective states, but also provides a sympathetic forum for everything from anti-gay activists, to opponents of a nuclear freeze, to apologists for big companies engaged in lucrative business with South Africa.

DIVISIONS AT THE CONGREGATIONAL LEVEL

What impact have these conflicts between liberals and conservatives had at the congregational level? Here, our evidence is sparse, but we do have some clues from both aggregate studies and case histories of

23. *Presbyterian Layman,* July/August 1988, p. 2.

particular congregations. At the aggregate level, we know from Gallup data that religious liberals and religious conservatives report having contact with members of the opposing faction in their local churches and even in Bible study groups and prayer fellowships. Although the numbers are small, this was true among Presbyterians just as it was in the sample as a whole.

The Gallup data also show that individuals who had made contact with the opposing faction in these local settings were almost as likely to hold negative views of their opponents as were those whose contact had come in less personal settings. Among those who identified themselves as religious liberals, 42 percent whose contact with conservatives had been in their current church held negative opinions of conservatives. Roughly the same proportions harbored negative sentiments when their contact had been in a Bibly study group or prayer fellowship. The only type of contacts that were associated with significantly higher levels of negative sentiment were contact in a former church and exposure to conservatives from reading or television.

Similar patterns were evident among persons who identified themselves as conservatives. Although differences in question wording made it impossible to compare the scope of negative sentiment toward liberals with that held by liberals toward conservatives, the evidence again pointed to the local church as one source of conflict. One-third of all conservatives who said they had come into contact with liberals in their current church held negative views of liberals; one-half of those whose contact had been in a previous church held negative views.[24]

A more detailed view of the dynamics of conflict in local congregations is available in R. Stephen Warner's valuable study of a Presbyterian church in Mendocino, California. Warner observed a congregation caught in the throes of a theological transition. Its character was vastly different at the end of the 1970s than it had been in the late 1960s. By happenstance, I had made a pilgrimage to this church myself in 1970. My impression, which Warner's retrospective research confirmed, was that the church sheltered a kind of bland Milquetoast liberalism that seemed to be all too common among small Presbyterian congregations in California in those days. A decade later it had become a vibrant home of evangelical fervor.

The change was relatively abrupt and involved some unusual

---

24. These results are from the 1984 national survey conducted by the Gallup Organization.

circumstances in the surrounding community. Evangelicalism triumphed, but not without difficulty. It triumphed by converting some, by bringing in new members, and above all by capturing the seat of power within the congregation and using it to bring in new leadership favorable to its cause. The new spirit was scarcely an evangelicalism of the radical right, but the liberal constituency found its worldview so much at odds with the new leadership that many found it impossible to stay in the congregation at all.[25]

In somewhat less dramatic fashion, but I suspect in a more typical way, the conflicts Warner observed were also evident in a church in New Jersey that I watched as both participant and observer between the mid-1970s and the mid-1980s. This was an independent community church, a grandchild, as it were, of Presbyterianism, whose own history provided an interesting commentary on the denomination. It was pastored by a minister whose training and sympathies lay in the Presbyterian tradition, in matters of both theology and church government. His grandfather had been the pastor of a leading Presbyterian church in New York City. His father had also been a Presbyterian minister, but had left the denomination in the 1950s, distraught by the liberal tendencies he saw developing, and started an independent church with the help of others sharing his concerns. The son's church was also independent, not so much in protest against Presbyterianism, but because its founders simply saw pragmatic advantages in remaining independent.

When I first came into contact with the congregation in the mid-1970s, shortly after its founding as a branch church in a new suburban community, it showed all the signs of having found a happy way of accommodating parishioners from both the right and left. The theological center of gravity was perhaps slightly to the right of Presbyterian churches in the area. But it was administered by a Presbyterian-style board of elders, accommodated people with differing views of the sacraments, and combined solid preaching with a strong commitment to fellowship, outreach, and service to the community. Leaders in the congregation varied in their personal views from strong supporters of the ACLU and the freeze movement to militant anticommunists.

Over the next decade, I witnessed this unity-amidst-diversity unravel. The congregation experienced in microcosm what was happening to the structure of American religion at large. Indeed, the pres-

---

25. R. Stephen Warner, *New Wine in Old Wineskins: Evangelicals and Liberals in a Small-Town Church* (Berkeley and Los Angeles: University of California Press, 1988).

sures from without—the impact of the nation's public religion—often contributed to the growing strife within. At first, during the Carter years, the increasing national popularity of the evangelical movement began to shape the congregation's policies: pressures for the pastor to align himself with the National Association of Evangelicals, increasing emphasis on church growth, speakers and tapes who reflected the sub-culture of American evangelicalism.

Then, for a time, the left, without consciously thinking of themselves as an alternative force, pushed the congregation to adopt its causes and orientations: upgrading the church's preaching and educational programs to better appeal to the surrounding intellectual and professional substratum of the community, publicly supporting the nuclear freeze, finding ways to bring racial diversity to the church, becoming involved in the Nestle boycott and starting a food cooperative, and eventually rethinking the church's position on gender and the role of women in leadership positions.

At about the same time, a countertendency began to appear on the right. With the intellectual and professional strata of the community remaining for the most part unchurched, the congregation grew primarily from the ranks of working-class tracts, older people, migrants from the Midwest and South, and professionals with little exposure to the liberal arts, especially business managers and engineers. Demands for basic Bible study rose from their ranks. Discussions of Jerry Falwell and other television preachers became more common. A local pregnancy clinic the church had supported began pressuring members to become politically active in the pro-life movement. Those who had pressed for gender equality were labeled "liberals" and "feminists." Increasingly, the congregation moved to the right, even to the point of refusing to participate in community services with churches whose denominations belonged to the National Council of Churches.

Today, this church remains the victim of the struggles it experienced in the early 1980s. Three ministers have come and gone. Many of the active members have gravitated either to churches more clearly to the right or to mainline churches more tolerant of diversity. Plans for a new building to accommodate an expected membership of a thousand have been postponed indefinitely. While new housing developments spring up all around it, the remaining congregation of two hundred members struggles to pay its debts and keep its parking lot free of weeds.

I do not mean to suggest that the tensions between religious liberals and religious conservatives are felt mainly at the congregational level or that they arise primarily from struggles within local churches. On the contrary, the survey evidence suggests, not surprisingly, that the tensions between religious liberals and religious conservatives are felt far more acutely at the national level than at the congregational level. National religious agencies, government, and the media seem to be the main foci of grievances.

For instance, among those in the national survey who held negative views of religious liberals, nearly half thought religious liberals had too much power in the media and in government, and four in ten thought liberals had too much power in national religious agencies; but fewer than one in ten thought religious liberals had too much power in local churches. The patterns among persons who held negative views of religious conservatives were similar, although less pronounced. Thus, approximately one-third of the respondents with anticonservative views thought conservatives had too much power in national religious agencies, government, and the media, while fewer than one-fourth thought conservatives had too much power in local churches.[26]

Some, I should note, have begun to argue that the tension between religious liberals and religious conservatives is now largely a thing of the past at the congregational level. Conflict is receding, they suggest, because conservatism is on the verge of triumph. Both the cases just cited suggest that this may be true, and anecdotal evidence provides ample support for this conclusion.

In many congregations, Bible study groups can be found that did not exist a decade ago. More emphasis is evident on Christian education for children and adults alike. Prayer fellowships have sprung up. Aggressively experimental forms of worship have been replaced by more conventional formats. And conservative laity have curbed the ambitions of their more liberally minded pastors and fellow laity, often resulting in retreats from such activities as gay rights, pro-choice movements, and the nuclear freeze.

How representative such anecdotal accounts may be is difficult to gauge: certainly the newspapers and rumor mills feed more on examples of new trends than on examples of old patterns simply repeating themselves. Some evidence from research studies points to the same conclusion, however. Particularly telling were the results of a

26. These results are based on my analysis of the 1984 Gallup data; the percentages reported are for 179 respondents who scored high on a scale of antiliberal attitudes and 288 respondents who scored high on a scale of anticonservative attitudes.

survey conducted in 1987 among 1,000 randomly selected Presbyterian congregations, from which 610 eventually returned questionnaires. When asked about the theological composition of their congregations, a majority of the elders surveyed said their congregations were moderately conservative.[27]

If we assume for the moment that the dominant tendency at the congregational level is in fact to the right, we then need to decipher some of the reasons why this trend may be taking place, and on that basis, come to a better understanding of how it may connect to the more public contours of religion in American society more broadly. One possibility that seems to have some empirical support is that elders themselves constitute a conservative force in local congregations. This is not to say that elders are any more conservative than pastors or other members in their social, political, or theological attitudes. If they are, their conservatism is at least selective. Thus, in recent studies, elders have given conservative responses in higher proportions than pastors and other lay members on issues such as supporting the Contras in Nicaragua and opposing a bilateral nuclear arms moratorium between the United States and the Soviet Union, and yet have shown no tendency toward greater conservatism on issues such as pornography and gender.[28]

Elders do, however, seem to worry more about how other parishioners will respond to change, and are somewhat less likely to want to risk initiating change. For example, a *Presbyterian Panel* survey found that elders were significantly more likely than pastors to predict a decline in church participation in their congregations if a woman were called as pastor. The study also showed that elders were less likely than pastors to say they would try to convince the congregation that a woman should be called, and more likely than pastors to say they would either take a neutral position or withdraw the woman's name and recommend a man.[29]

Some evidence also suggests that elders may be relatively less supportive of the work of the regional and national offices of the denomination, which have often come under attack as being too liberal. For instance, in a recent survey of attitudes toward stewardship, elders were less than half as likely as pastors to say that supporting the mis-

27. Study conducted by the Research Unit of the Support Agency of the Presbyterian Church, a brief report of which was published in *The Presbyterian Layman*, November/December 1987, p. 1.

28. See, for example, responses to the various questions reported in the *Presbyterian Panel*, March 1987, and September 1987.

29. *Presbyterian Panel*, September 1986, pp. A3, A4.

sion activities of the presbytery, synod, and General Assembly should be a very important reason for financial giving, and were even less likely to give this response than the average member.[30] Whether it reflects their own disposition or simply their views of what is best for the congregation, then, elders may actually be one of the active factors moving local congregations toward a more conservative posture.

Other tendencies—ones that we can infer at least from broader studies of religious commitment in American life—also point toward a strengthening of the conservative orientation. One is that much of the fervor of the 1960s and 1970s, the fervor of social activism and experimentation that figured in the liberalism of the period, has been displaced by narrower, more materialistic concerns, and the political climate of the nation has shifted considerably toward a platform of strong defense, nostalgia for the past, individualism, family, and traditional morality. Another is that rising levels of education appear to be associated not only with more liberal views on many theological questions, but also with defection from organized religion entirely. Consequently, the numeric increases in college-educated persons in the United States do not necessarily translate into active, committed leadership with liberal orientations in the churches. Furthermore, by its very nature, theological liberalism has championed diversity and the sanctity of alternative quests for the divine in a way that sometimes undercuts strong appeals to stay loyal to the local church and become a booster of its programs.

There are, however, two tendencies that help replenish and keep active the liberal wing of the Presbyterian Church. One is the role of women. My research suggests that in most denominations women with college educations are only modestly more likely to be active in their churches than women in the same denominations without college educations; when college-educated women hold feminist views, their church participation is considerably lower. This pattern is not the case among Presbyterian women, though. Presbyterian women with at least some college education are twice as likely to attend church regularly as Presbyterian women with no college training (the proportions are 50 percent and 25 percent, respectively).[31]

30. *Presbyterian Panel,* June 1987, p. A2.
31. These results are from my analysis of General Social Survey Data collected between 1972 and 1984; the percentages are based on 117 Presbyterian women with at least some college education and 162 Presbyterian women with no college education; among Presbyterian men, no statistically significant difference in church attendance is present between those with or without college educations.

The data also show that Presbyterian women who gave feminist responses to attitude questions were no less likely to attend church regularly than were Presbyterian women who gave more traditional responses.[32] If these results are valid, they suggest that women with more education and with sympathy to the feminist movement—that is, women most likely to share sympathies with liberal views on other social and religious issues—are likely to remain active in the church. Moreover, the numbers of these women may in fact increase as more and more women attain higher education and adopt gender-egalitarian values.

It is also instructive to speculate about why this pattern holds in the Presbyterian Church and not in most other denominations. Two characteristics of Presbyterian women stand out. A relatively high proportion overall do have at least some college training (in these data, 42 percent did, compared with an average of only 25 percent for all Protestant women), and a relatively high proportion hold gender-egalitarian values (58 percent compared with 42 percent among Protestant women as a whole). In short, Presbyterian women with these characteristics are likely to feel they have kindred spirits in their congregations, and for this reason, they may feel more comfortable remaining active in these congregations. This interpretation is, incidentally, supported by patterns evident in the two other traditions in which better-educated women with feminist orientations constitute a significant share of the population: among Episcopal and Jewish women. In both these traditions, higher levels of education and feminist orientations were positively associated with religious involvement.

The other social characteristic that augurs well for the liberal wing of Presbyterianism is the fact that denominational switching follows, to some extent, educational distinctions. Several examples will illustrate. If we look at persons in national surveys who were raised in Baptist churches but are no longer members of Baptist churches, about 10 percent of those who have been to college switch to Presbyterian churches, while the figure among those who have not been to college is only 5 percent. Similarly, if we look at former Methodists, 11 percent of the college-educated group have become Presbyterians, while only 6 percent of the noncollege group have. Among persons who formerly belonged to Protestant sects, 15 percent of those with college

---

32. Specifically, 30 percent of the women who scored high on a scale of feminist attitudes said they attended church nearly every week or more often, compared with 31 percent of the women who scored low on the scale.

educations have become Presbyterians, while only 5 percent of those without college educations have become Presbyterians. In other words, the Presbyterian church draws better-educated members who leave other denominations more than it does less-educated persons. In general, higher levels of education are strongly associated with more liberal theological, social, and political views. Thus, it seems reasonable to infer that the Presbyterian Church is gaining some members from other denominations who are switching from a more conservative environment to one in which they can feel more comfortable.[33]

PROSPECTS FOR RECONCILIATION

Although there may be some possibility that the division between Presbyterian liberals and Presbyterian conservatives will be healed simply by the triumph of the latter, I believe the evidence on the whole points more toward a continuation of this division. It is, of course, rooted to some extent in reactions to policies of the denomination and the secular arena. Major shifts in these policies, say, a Supreme Court decision reversing *Roe* v. *Wade*, or a major war in Central America, could alter the terms of discussion considerably. But the strife between Presbyterian liberals and conservatives has deeper roots than concerns about these specific issues. It reflects broader currents in the society; the mass media fan the flames of contention whenever a new scandal erupts among religious broadcasters; political candidates and right-wing special purpose groups find it is to their advantage to levy direct-mail campaigns at religious audiences; and within Presbyterianism itself, too many special purpose groups have become organized to let controversy simply fade from view.

The cleavage between liberal and conservative Presbyterians is, in my view, both serious and unfortunate. Although it may, at its best, ensure that different points of view are heard in denominational bureaucracies, it has become a means to an end that often overshadows the end itself. Certainly, the biblical image of love, or more modern ideals of community and reconciliation, are difficult to see amidst the turmoil that divides liberals and conservatives.

This division should not, however, be blamed for the numeric

33. These results are from my analysis of General Social Survey data collected between 1972 and 1984; they are based on more than 700 cases of former Baptists, 800 cases of former Methodists, and 500 cases of former members of Protestant sects.

problems Presbyterians have been facing over the past two decades. To the contrary, the mobilization of conservatives has probably checked some of the numeric drift the denomination has experienced. Other factors, including increases in average age, lower birth rates, higher levels of education, more and more women entering the labor market, and geographic sunk costs in the location of local churches, probably account for this drift more effectively than does the contention between liberals and conservatives.

At the same time, the numeric losses of the denomination should not become an excuse for each side attempting to impute blame to the other side and engaging in activities that damn the enemy within. In a shrinking religious market, acrimony of this kind is all too easy to give vent to. Conservatives can make their voice heard more loudly if they proclaim declining numbers to be the result of gay clergy, the murderous immorality of pro-choice activists, unreasonable criticisms of wealthy contributors to the church, and a wishy-washy stand on biblical authority. Liberals can gain temporary satisfaction by convincing themselves that conservative denominations are waging a conspiratorial war against the Presbyterian Church to steal its members. But neither kind of allegation has been substantiated with solid empirical evidence. Even if it were, a war to the bitter end is not only likely to drain the denomination's resources even more but also runs contrary to the doctrines of love and reconciliation that lie at the core of Christianity.

Despite the issues over which liberal and conservative Presbyterians currently disagree, on many other issues common ground could easily be found. Love of God, love of neighbor, the reality of sin, and the need for forgiveness and faith still constitute theological cornerstones on which structures of unity can be built. Even more controversial issues often evoke more consensus than might be expected. For example, more than three-quarters of all members now say it would make no difference to them whether a man or a woman performed such pastoral activities as preaching, administering the Lord's Supper, or performing a baptism.[34] Better than 80 percent favor a total ban on movies and tapes that depict sexual violence; nearly the same proportion regards portrayals of sexual violence as a violation of a woman's civil rights; and yet the overwhelming majority of Presbyterians uphold the right to freedom of speech in other areas.[35]

34. *Presbyterian Panel*, September 1986, p. A14.
35. *Presbyterian Panel*, September 1987, p. A9.

On other issues, broad consensus exists on basic theological principles, even though disagreements are present on specific means of implementing these principles. Peacemaking provides a vivid illustration. As already mentioned, Presbyterians remain sorely divided over questions of nuclear disarmament, aid to Nicaraguan rebels, the Star Wars initiative, and so on. Nevertheless, virtually all Presbyterians agree that peacemaking should in one way or another be an important concern of the church. Eighty percent agree that "Peacemaking is not simply 'another political issue' but is a central declaration of the Gospel"; and 86 percent agree with the statement, "Because God is at work throughout the world granting peace, Christians join God as peacemakers in families, communities and in the international arena."[36] In short, there is a basis on which to build toward consensus.

The path toward greater harmony among Presbyterians, though, does not run simply through the sunny meadow of common ground. Consensual issues perhaps need to be emphasized more than they have been in the past. But focusing on areas of agreement will not in itself overcome the areas of serious disagreement. Instead of trying to deny the existence of division, Presbyterians need to explore alternative paths toward genuine reconciliation.

One path is what sociologists call insulation. Special purpose groups organize around single issues and simply go their own way. At the congregational level, the gay task force meets on Tuesday evenings and the charismatic fellowship meets on Wednesdays. A semblance of reconciliation is present because the two constituencies never really have to meet together. At the denominational level, at least some of the many special purpose groups that have appeared in the past two decades probably serve this function as well. Their appearance has created a way of containing conflict by giving it organizational expression.

To their credit, special purpose groups may well encourage diversity and permit a variety of opinions to be expressed and interests to be recognized. The various boards and task forces that have considered the rules regulating special organizations in the Presbyterian Church have always recognized the important role these organizations play in maintaining diversity and in voicing dissent. However, the same regulations have always stressed the importance of such groups functioning in a way that genuine dialogue is encouraged, peace and unity of the church is maintained, and the larger mission of the denomination is upheld.[37]

---

36. *Presbyterian Panel,* March 1987, p. A2.

On all three counts, special purpose groups have shown signs of moving in directions that leave much to be desired. If exchanges of emotion-laden rhetoric in church periodicals constitute dialogue, then the special purpose groups have indeed met one of these criteria. If dialogue involves efforts to arrive at understanding and agreement, however, little has been accomplished. At minimum, more attention needs to be devoted to examining the assumptions behind alternative positions, and to striving for greater clarity about the issues, rather than pressing simply for the superiority of one's position. Moreover, peace and unity within the church appears largely to have been sacrificed to other concerns. Nuclear disarmament or outlawing abortion may indeed appear to be far more serious to the survival of our nation than peace and unity within the church. But if the latter is not pursued seriously, it is doubtful that the church will have any special authority with which to voice its claims on more specific issues of national concern. There is also much room for redirecting the balance between special organizations and the mission of the church itself. Too often, the strident voices of special purpose groups have become the church's primary witness to the wider world. This is not surprising in an era when the mass media increasingly set the agenda for national politics and constantly seek out controversy to fill their headlines. But the mission of the church may need to be pursued in quieter ways as well: through the ministry of local congregations in local neighborhoods, through personal interaction and caring, and through the leavening influence of the gospel itself manifested in word and deed.

A second path toward reconciliation is the legislative model that the denomination has practiced since its inception. Whenever genuine differences of opinion appear, task forces are set in motion to study the matter, and then reports are filed, the General Assembly evokes the collective will, and on serious issues decisions are sent down to local presbyteries again for final ratification. This model is likely to continue, but it needs to be monitored carefully to prevent it from simply exacerbating the problem.

Legislative politics, like special purpose groups, has been widely hailed as an effective means to include everyone in the governing process. When people have a chance to make their voice heard, if only indirectly through their elected representatives, the decisions their government—or denomination—makes are supposed to be legitimate.

37. See, for example, Walter J. Ungerer, "What is the Future of Chapter IX Groups?" *Presbyterian Communique*, March/April 1988, pp. 1, 12, 14.

One may disagree with the outcome, but still the procedure by which the outcome is decided ensures that person's compliance.

This at least is the theory behind the form of representative government that Presbyterians and many other American denominations have adopted. It has often served these denominations well. In a period when more and more of our lives are influenced by the legislative process at the national level, though, the limitations of this model in the religious sphere need to be recognized clearly. In the religious sphere, more than in the political sphere, it is limited by the balance that must always be maintained between two forms of legitimation: what social theorists refer to as "procedural rationality," on the one hand, and "ethical rationality," on the other hand. Procedural rationality has developed gradually in modern secular societies such as our own in which no authority higher than the people itself is recognized. Thus, we say a law is legitimate if the proper procedures have been followed in initiating and passing it. In contrast, ethical rationality recognizes absolute standards, moral principles, or truths that may or may not be served by proper procedures. Thus, a resolution can be passed by the General Assembly of the Presbyterian Church, having met all the denomination's procedural rules, and still be regarded by many Presbyterians as illegitimate because it violates their sense of divine truth. Of course, this is not merely a hypothetical example; it attests to the limitations of the legislative model, especially at a time when the church is deeply divided over many basic theological orientations.

The legislative model also confronts special limitations when policy deliberations become objects of acrimony among special interest groups. Testimony to this effect has been amply provided by the widely read book *Habits of the Heart*.[38] When Robert Bellah and his colleagues asked people to talk about American politics, they found many respondents expressing feelings of distance, alienation, and disengagement. This reaction was no surprise, but the reasons behind these feelings were especially revealing. People felt alienated, not simply because politics was removed from their personal lives and conducted in distant legislative halls, but also because it was seen as a nasty business involving incessant conflict. People withdrew from it because they wanted harmony in their lives. Perhaps the same tendency applies to the church. When church politics become acrimonious and conflictual,

---

38. Robert N. Bellah, et al., *Habits of the Heart* (Berkeley and Los Angeles: University of California Press, 1985).

there is surely a tendency for some to say simply, "A plague on both your houses; I will simply believe in my own quiet, private way."

The legislative model is also limited in religious settings because of the presence of denominational pluralism in American society. Should one happen to disagree on ethical grounds with the procedures that the government uses to implement legislation, one can of course exit the system and move to another country. But this prospect is unlikely. It involves serious uprooting: selling the house, finding a different job, going through immigration, and perhaps learning a new language. Such barriers do not exist in the world of competing denominations. Leaving one religious tradition for another is, as we have seen, altogether common. Furthermore, it has become virtually impossible in the modern world to live without citizenship in some country, but increasing numbers of people live without membership in any of our nation's major denominations. To this extent, therefore, the legislative model can be used to reconcile some of the divisions that arise in religious settings, but it seems an unlikely candidate for advancing reconciliation at any fundamental level.

A third path toward reconciliation is the way of compassion. To a greater extent than either of the other two, the way of compassion requires efforts not only to understand one's opponents' views but to identify with the suffering of one's opponent. It demands that the Good Samaritan's example of love be applied not only to the man beaten and lying by the road but also to the opponent one faces over the conference table or to the antagonist one reads about in the newspaper.

Although the way of compassion may have the strongest links with biblical tradition, I would be the last one to argue that it, rather than the way of insulation or legislation, is the only true method of achieving reconciliation. All three have their place. They represent, in a broad sense, the paths of passion, reason, and caring. Passion is needed because the issues about which Presbyterians and members of other denominations are concerned are indeed matters of high importance to our lives as individuals and as a society. Reason, as exemplified in the legislative model of church government, is an established method of arriving at the best means of accomplishing the objectives that passion sets before us. And compassion takes the edge off the issues we are passionate about, adds feeling to the dictates of reason, and upholds the importance of community among those with whom we disagree as well as among those with whom we agree. Each has its place in the practical task of pursuing the elusive ideal of reconciliation.

Part II   DYNAMICS OF THE SECULAR

Five

Civil Privatism
and the State

THE EXPANDING SOCIAL ROLE of the modern welfare state has become a topic of increasing importance, not only to policymakers in the secular sphere, but also to those who seek a better understanding of American religion. As discussed in chapter 1, our churches are a central component of the voluntary sector in American society, but this voluntary sector exists largely at the mercy of the political and economic sectors. As the other sectors change, religion is forced to adapt. One of the major changes that has taken place in the political sector has been the steady growth of government functions. Today, government is involved in nearly every dimension of our lives.

Social scientists have investigated many important aspects of state expansion: national variations in welfare expenditures, state-level variations in governmental redistribution programs, the timing of early adoption of national pension programs, and the growth of various forms of state bureaucracy, to name a few.[1] In addition to these rela-

---

1. See, for example, Nancy DiTomaso, "Class Politics and Public Bureaucracy: The U.S. Department of Labor," in *Classes, Class Conflict, and the State,* ed. Maurice Zeitlin (Cambridge, MA: Winthrop, 1980), pp. 135-52; Alexander Hicks, "The Political Economy of Redistribution in the American States," in *Classes, Class Conflict, and the State,* pp. 217-36; Alexander Hicks, Roger Friedland, and Edwin Johnson, "Class Power and State Policy: The Case of Large Business Corporations, Labor Unions and Governmental Redistribution in the American States," *American Sociological Review* 43 (1978): 302-

tively straightforward aspects of the welfare state itself, another ramification of state expansion that has been discussed extensively in the
theoretical literature is the role of state expansion in eroding voluntary participation in secondary groups, including participation in
churches—the process that Jürgen Habermas has described as "civil
privatism."[2] This alleged effect of state expansion has been given special attention in the theoretical literature because participation in voluntary associations has typically been regarded as an essential component
of the strength of democratic societies.

In capsule, Habermas argues that contradictions inherent in
the role of the state in advanced capitalist societies lead to an observ-
able retreat from membership in organizations that link individuals to
the public sphere and that facilitate the articulation of public "will formation." Habermas is concerned with the full range of independent
sector organizations that perform these functions directly or that contribute to their fulfillment indirectly: not only political action groups
but also churches, schools, community agencies, and fraternal organizations that provide spheres of "communicative action" about
public values. As the state expands, citizens presumably become less
involved in these kinds of voluntary organizations.

Although this is but one of several manifestations of civil
privatism (subjective narcissism often being mentioned as another), it
presumably constitutes one of the more significant societal effects of
the growth of the bureaucratic welfare state. In the absence of such
voluntary organizational involvements, individuals are said to become
increasingly removed from the public sphere and turn to other interests, chiefly the personal gratifications of mass consumption, atomized
leisure activities, and an attenuated version of family intimacy.

Moreover, the consequences of civil privatism are said to be
largely negative for the maintenance of democracy. An atomized
citizenry is likely to be subjected more easily to political repression
since nongovernmental organizations capable of resisting repression
are absent or weak. Also likely, it is claimed, is a narrowing of the

---

15; Ann Shola Orloff and Theda Skocpol, "Why Not Equal Protection? Explaining the
Politics of Public Social Spending in Britain, 1900-1911, and the United States, 1880s-
1920," *American Sociological Review* 49 (1984): 726-50; Jill S. Quadagno, "Welfare Capitalism and the Social Security Act of 1935," *American Sociological Review* 49 (1984): 632-47;
and Harold Wilensky, *The Welfare State and Equality: Structural and Ideological Roots of Public
Expenditures* (Berkeley and Los Angeles: University of California Press, 1975).
        2. Jürgen Habermas, *Legitimation Crisis,* tr. Thomas McCarthy (Boston: Beacon
Press, 1975).

state's interests and an eventual weakening of its capacity to govern. Lacking effective means of organizing and of articulating larger questions about values and societal goals, the public loses interest in the state and potentially perceives it with a lack of confidence or fails to accord it legitimacy. In response, the state may resort increasingly to programs that appeal to the lowest-common-denominator values remaining among individuals oriented toward mass consumption and private leisure—that is, the promotion of economic growth. Ironically, social observers also suggest, the very social welfare programs that were taken over from the private sector by the state may thereby become jeopardized as the state seeks to reduce its costs sufficiently to stimulate economic expansion.[3]

For all of these reasons, then, the relation between state expansion and civil privatism has been of considerable theoretical interest. Yet equally plausible arguments can also be marshalled against the thesis that state expansion generates civil privatism.

In this chapter I survey the arguments relating state expansion and civil privatism. I also present counterarguments that cast doubt on the inevitability of state expansion resulting in civil privatism. Set in opposition to one another, these arguments reveal the importance of adducing testable empirical assertions. Next, I further specify the arguments by considering them in relation to the current situation in American religion. I then develop some indicators of the relevant aspects of these arguments and demonstrate their relations for the United States in 1952 and 1981.

DOES STATE EXPANSION LEAD TO CIVIL PRIVATISM?

A century and a half ago, Tocqueville established the basic framework for the present debate over civil privatism by suggesting a close relationship between democratic government in the United States and voluntary civic associations. Americans' penchant for engaging in voluntary associations was, in Tocqueville's view, a decisive factor inhibiting tendencies toward repressive government. Churches, charitable organizations, civic groups, and community associations, he argued, all provided a way of articulating private interests and values and of mobilizing the populace to bring pressure on elected

---

3. Gianfranco Poggi, *The Development of the Modern State* (Stanford: Stanford University Press, 1978), pp. 146-47.

representatives in behalf of these interests, and more generally, of nurturing communal bonds and collective sentiments of moral responsibility. Tocqueville warned, however, that the growth of the state could interfere with these associations and lead individuals to withdraw from them: "It is easy to foresee that the time is drawing near when man will be less and less able to produce, by himself alone, the commonest necessaries of life. The task of the governing power will therefore perpetually increase, and its very efforts will extend it every day. The more it stands in the place of associations, the more will individuals, losing the notion of combining together, require its assistance: these are causes and effects that unceasingly create each other."[4]

In Tocqueville's time the balance between governmental activities and voluntary associations tended strongly toward the latter. Indeed, voluntary associations were to grow considerably in strength and in number during the course of the nineteenth century.

By the middle of the twentieth century, however, new concerns over the nature of this balance were beginning to be raised. An atomized "mass society" of individuals bound together only by mass media, and therefore subject to propagandist appeals and totalitarian manipulation, was alleged to be in the making. In these discussions, however, it was not the state but tendencies in the broader society, particularly urbanization, population change, and economic diversification, that were assumed to be responsible for the emerging signs of erosion in the strength of voluntary associations. As the society became more complex, individuals would apparently become increasingly disinclined to participate in their churches, civic associations, and neighborhood groups.

The more recent formulations by Habermas and others are distinctive, therefore, in attributing the growth of civil privatism primarily to the expansion of the state itself. For example, Nicos Poulantzas emphasizes the state's role in undercutting village, regional, and kin-based collectivities, and in transforming these collectivities into aggregates of isolated, autonomous individuals.[5] Similarly, Robert Bellah and associates present a normative argument which envisions conscious strengthening of voluntary associations as the most effective

---

4. Alexis de Tocqueville, *Democracy in America*, 2 vols. (New York: Vintage Books, 1945), 2:116.

5. Nicos Poulantzas, *State, Power, Socialism* (London: NLB, 1978); for a brief summary of this argument, see Martin Carnoy, *The State and Political Theory* (Princeton: Princeton University Press, 1984), pp. 112-21.

means of restraining what they call "the pull toward administrative despotism."[6]

Habermas's own discussion of civil privatism is, regrettably, framed largely in terms of subjective conceptions. Rather than addressing the issue primarily as a relevant feature of the "legitimation crisis" confronting the modern state, he considers it chiefly as the principal manifestation of crisis at the social-psychological or *motivational* level. The questions he raises have more to do with the capacity of a privatized worldview to withstand other cultural and societal changes than with the effects of state expansion on civil privatism. Nevertheless, his discussion is able to take this direction only because he takes it for granted that state expansion does in fact result in a tendency to withdraw from participation in voluntary organizations. Having made this assumption, he then goes on to argue that this kind of withdrawal has been functional, at least in the short term, for maintaining the stability of the modern state. In questioning whether tendencies such as scientism, universalism, and postauratic art create cognitive dissonances with the subjective components of civil privatism, he is in essence addressing the issue of whether the functional aspects of civil privatism are likely to be transmuted at the same time that the state continues to require these functions.

It is clear, even from Habermas's discussion of the subjective components of civil privatism, that the vitality of voluntary associations bears critically on the issue of civil privatism. Voluntary associations are assumed to facilitate participation in the public sphere, and therefore to inhibit the spread of civil privatism, both directly and indirectly. Their direct role is as collective entities which, though frequently organized around purely apolitical activities, may from time to time participate directly in the political system, mobilizing collective action on the part of members or using bureaucratic resources to bring pressure to bear on the state. Lobbying efforts by religious denominations or the formation of political action movements, such as Moral Majority, by religious leaders would serve as examples. The indirect role of voluntary organizations is to mobilize individuals for political participation by bringing them into contact with others, broadening their sphere of concerns, and providing them with resources such as interpersonal skills and information. Research has, in fact, shown positive

6. Robert Bellah, et al., *Habits of the Heart* (Berkeley and Los Angeles: University of California Press, 1984), p. 211.

effects of involvement in voluntary associations on simple political participation measures such as voter turnout.[7]

Closer consideration of the foregoing arguments does, however, reveal a number of ambiguities. Habermas's discussion is cast largely in functionalist terms: civil privatism is functional for the modern welfare state because it prevents citizens from becoming aware of the inherent contradictions in this kind of state. But this argument by itself does not specify the mechanisms by which civil privatism might come about; thus, from an empirical standpoint, the possibility has to be left open that civil privatism might not actually result from state expansion even though the society would somehow be served if it did. Bellah's argument, focusing on the normative importance of voluntary associations, seems to assume that such associations can be maintained *despite* expansion of the state.

Even Tocqueville's scattered remarks on the subject are less than straightforward. He argues that states attempt to curb political associations by prohibiting them and by bringing them within the orbit of governmental regulations; and this attempt to control, he suggests, is likely to erode the strength of other, nonpolitical associations. But he also suggests that governments may not envision civil associations as a curb on their own powers and may indeed try to encourage these associations, especially if they are ostensibly nonpolitical: "[Governments] bear a natural goodwill to civil associations . . . because they readily discover that instead of directing the minds of the community to public affairs these institutions serve to divert them from such reflections."[8] Seemingly, therefore, governments may find it in their interest to promote civil associations.

Some aspects of the more general argument have also been examined empirically, with negative results. One study casts doubt on the view that mass education in the United States (which Habermas and others take as an agent of privatization) came about because of an expanding state bureaucracy.[9] Doubt has also been cast on the general

7. See, for example, Marvin Olson, "Social Participation and Voting Turnout: A Multivariate Analysis," *American Sociological Review* 37 (1972): 317-32. The importance of voluntary associations to the concept of civil privatism is also underscored by the fact that subjective measures, which conceive of privatism simply as an attitude, have generally *not* shown relations with political participation; see, for example, Susan Hansen, Linda Franz, and Margaret Netemeyer-Mays, "Women's Political Participation and Policy Preferences," *Social Science Quarterly* 56 (1976): 101-10; and Virginia Shapiro, *The Political Integration of Women* (Urbana: University of Illinois Press, 1983).

8. *Democracy in America,* 2:126.

9. John W. Meyer, David Tyack, Joane Nagel, and Audri Gordon, "Public

thesis of a negative relation between welfare state expansion and the strength of voluntarism by a study comparing the origins of welfare policies in Britain and the United States.[10] This study suggests, however, that voluntarism was not the primary impediment to the early development of social welfare policies in the United States; it does not speculate on whether the welfare state, once in place, erodes voluntary associations as it expands.

QUESTIONING THE STATE'S EFFECTS ON CIVIL PRIVATISM

As opposed to merely raising critical questions, another line of argumentation suggests that state expansion does not result in an inevitable tendency toward civil privatism. Indeed, these arguments suggest that state expansion may actually encourage participation in voluntary organizations. Also rooted in the Tocquevillian legacy, this strand of theory engages sociology primarily through the classic work of Emile Durkheim, followed by that of Robert Nisbet, and more recently by a more scattered group of contributors. While sensitive to the atomizing tendencies in industrialized societies, this line of argument accords the voluntary sector sufficient institutional strength (at least in the United States) to resist totalitarian political pressures, and argues that the capacity of the modern democratic state to govern under conditions of increased complexity in fact *requires* a mutually accommodating relation between the state and private associations. As Nisbet observes, "intermediary associations and the spontaneous social groups which compose society, rather than atomized political particles, become the prime units of theoretical and practical consideration."[11]

In this conception, the modern welfare state remains but *one* of many politically relevant associations. While it may command the greatest resources and pursue interests reflecting its own organizational characteristics, the state is nevertheless conceived of primarily as an arbiter among a plurality of interest groups. For the state to govern well, it must encourage the viability of these groups and maintain a

---

Education as Nation-Building in America: Enrollments and Bureaucratization in the American States, 1870-1930," *American Journal of Sociology* 85 (1979): 591-613.

10. Orloff and Skocpol, *American Sociological Review* 49 (1984): 726-50.

11. Robert A. Nisbet, *Community and Power* (Oxford: Oxford University Press, 1962), p. 250.

balance among them, rather than letting individuals become atomized and therefore susceptible to recruitment by totalitarian parties.

From this point of view, the erosion of voluntary and other communal associations tends to be linked mainly with processes in the larger environment, such as urbanization and geographic mobility, while the state is regarded as being dependent upon, and therefore the promoter of, some form of mediating social structures. The state may become unstable, even to the point of being subverted by totalitarianism, if the public becomes atomized and apathetic, so state officials find it in their long-term interest to foster the development of secondary associations. These associations provide channels for the state to use, then, in implementing policies, and they protect the long-run interests of the state by helping it to adapt to, and incorporate resources from, the changing social environment.[12]

In many of the more traditional versions of this argument, the primary guardians of voluntary associations in the face of advancing state bureaucratization were said to be a love of freedom and a collective interest in maintaining democracy. Thus, the dominant tendency built into the social structure itself remains that of civil privatism, while ideals and values were seen as the only available brakes on this tendency. To suggest that civil privatism is not the wave of the future, therefore, required adopting a rather heroic, hopeful vision of the power of ideals to resist structural tendencies. More recent formulations, however, have begun to specify processes related to the state itself that may serve as self-correcting tendencies against the onslaught of civil privatism.

One argument can be derived from the literature on internal colonialism. Although various reformulations of this literature have been made, the relevant contribution in the present context stems from the insight that expansive state bureaucracies may be able to administer more effectively, not by atomizing the population, but by enlisting the assistance of collectivities. In this view, the maintenance of strong secondary group identities may actually be promoted by the state, rather than merely being a residual left over from the past. Since much of the specific work on internal colonization has focused on naturally occurring ascriptive collectivities, especially ethnic groups, its relevance to the privatization literature has generally been overlooked.

---

12. This argument is made in Peter L. Berger and Richard Neuhaus, *To Empower People: The Role of Mediating Structures in Public Policy* (Washington, D.C.: American Enterprise Institute, 1977).

However, some of the added considerations that have emerged from this work lend it greater relevance. For example, one writer has recast the discussion of ethnic solidarity in a political mobilization framework, suggesting specifically that ethnic groups' potential for mobilization depends heavily on leadership resources, such as an educated elite.[13] By extension, it may be argued that one of the more general by-products of state expansion is an enlarged pool of alienable resources that may contribute to the maintenance and success of voluntary associations. Educated leadership is but one example.

Another mechanism by which state expansion may encourage the growth of voluntary associations is by defining more and more of life as "public issues." As Harvard sociologist Daniel Bell has observed, the advancing role of government seems to remove whole categories of decision making from the marketplace and from the private individual by redefining them as "group rights."[14] Thus, questions of personal taste become issues of social justice; morality is superseded by civil liberties; individual interests, by demands for collective entitlement; and so on. He suggests that the end result is a proliferation of involvement in both old and new associations, in ascriptive as well as voluntary groups, in order to lay claims on the state. Paradoxically, this tendency may even be accompanied by a subjective turn toward "bourgeois hedonism" (i.e., narcissism) at the individual level, because group interests and private wants are not necessarily incompatible.

In states with a well-developed set of voluntary associations, such as the United States, these organizations may be able to exert a sufficient amount of pressure on the state, despite overall increases in state activities, to ensure a substantial role for themselves in articulating public policy. Pressures to maintain tax exemption for churches and other nonprofit voluntary associations afford a clear example. Although these exemptions have often been gained at the cost of promises not to engage in political activities, some concessions have been granted. Under the 1976 Tax Reform Act, for example, many categories of charitable organizations were allowed to spend up to 20 percent of their total expenditures on direct lobbying without being taxed. For this and other reasons, it has not been uncommon for voluntary associations to mount efforts aimed at influencing the state and at maintaining their own strength in the face of state expansion.

13. See Eric M. Leifer, "Competing Models of Political Mobilization: The Role of Ethnic Ties," *American Journal of Sociology* 87 (1977): 23-47.

14. Daniel Bell, *The Cultural Contradictions of Capitalism* (New York: Basic Books, 1976), pp. 194-99.

Finally, the expansion of the welfare state, chiefly in the area of providing public services, may not occur strictly at the expense of voluntary associations, because the definition of "services" is itself expandable. For example, state financing of higher education has grown enormously since World War II, but private colleges and universities have experienced only a relative, rather than an absolute, decline because of the overall expansion of the system of higher education more generally. Broadened conceptions of the rights of handicapped persons, children, minority groups, and the aged have not only resulted in state expansion but in new opportunities for voluntary agencies. Insofar as many of these extensions in conceptions of rights and entitlement have involved the state in some way, voluntary associations have also tended to mobilize sectors of the population for participation in policy discussions. During the debate over the Equal Rights Amendment, for example, many conservative religious organizations launched special programs to mobilize opposition to the proposal.

In short, plausible arguments can be mustered both in favor of and in opposition to the hypothesis that state expansion inevitably leads to an increase in the kind of civil privatism suggested by declining strength of voluntary associations. The issue is clearly an empirical question. It is, however, an issue that must be delimited before an empirical examination can be considered. Some kinds of voluntary associations may be adversely affected by state expansion, while others are not. As the foregoing discussion has implied, different outcomes may be expected depending on the institutional resources of the kind of voluntary association at issue as well as its capacity to reap benefit from the by-products resulting from state expansion.

CIVIL PRIVATISM AND THE STRENGTH OF RELIGION

Religion has often been identified as a particularly important sphere in which to observe the process of privatization; indeed, various formulations of the civil privatism thesis more generally have been especially prominent in the theoretical literature on modern religion. Some aspects of the expansionary state that might contribute to declining involvement in religious organizations have been discussed, but most of this literature has focused on other potential sources of civil privatism, such as the anonymity of urban life, the effects of declining interfaith competition for the religious market, or vague conceptions of the corrosive effects of modernity. It is necessary, therefore, to rely mainly on more general discussions of the state for arguments that might be applicable to religion.

The position of religion in relation to the public/private distinction has always been ambiguous. In some formulations the historic establishment of a formal wall of separation in the United States between church and state has led observers to regard religion as strictly private. One student of the modern state writes: "Matters of creed and cult [were] the first to be claimed as 'private' with respect to the state, as proper for the state to ignore or to safeguard impartially."[15] To assert that religion is formally in the private sector is, however, not meant to imply that it has been thoroughly "privatized," that is, become an example of atomized, consumption-oriented civil privatism. To the contrary, religious organizations have been widely seen as an example of the kinds of civic associations in which citizens' values are mobilized and brought to bear on the public sphere. In Tocqueville's view, for example, churches were one of the mainstays of American democracy.

The question of whether American religion tends more toward active involvement in the public sphere or leads to privatistic withdrawal has been examined empirically. The available data, while demonstrating that some privatizing tendencies are evident, clearly establishes that the predominant tendency has been one of *encouraging* civic involvement. Some of the evidence is direct; other evidence is inferential, but it uniformly supports the assumption that religious membership and involvement can be regarded as a contributor to the public sphere. Not only do studies demonstrate positive relations at the individual level between church membership and voting, voter registration, and participation in political campaigns, but religious organizations have also been frequent actors on the political stage as collectivities as well, mobilizing demonstrations and boycotts, lobbying and endorsing legislation, and issuing pronouncements on a wide variety of contemporary issues.

The main arguments that point to a negative relationship between state expansion and voluntary religious membership focus on the state's arrogation of social functions that were formerly performed to some significant degree by the churches. These functions include education, welfare services, and the enforcement of public safety. In each of these areas evidence indicates that the churches were, in fact, actively involved until recent decades. At the end of World War II, for

15. Poggi, *The Development of the Modern State*, p. 150.

example, the Methodists alone operated 77 colleges and universities; the Presbyterians, 71 colleges; and the Southern Baptists, 53 colleges and junior colleges. According to a national study done prior to the war, religious organizations controlled approximately one-third of all endowments for higher education.[16] Welfare services were also an important branch of religious activity, but varied greatly in different locales. In some communities less than one percent of religious expenditures in the 1930s went for welfare or relief; in contrast, a study of St. Louis prior to the Depression had shown that 37 percent of all welfare services were under religious auspices.[17] A national estimate in 1929 showed that Protestant churches operated between 275 and 350 hospitals (15 percent of the national total) and 250 to 325 homes for the aged (42 percent of the total).[18] Religion's role in providing for public safety was less easily measured, but churches were widely regarded as the guardians of basic moral principles undergirding law and order. Community studies in the 1930s and 1940s found clergy actively involved in a wide variety of local skirmishes over such issues as movie theaters, gambling, and the use of alcohol. Thus these kinds of services were among the ways in which churches attempted to influence social affairs, and they provided incentives for people to become church members and to contribute to the maintenance of religious organizations.

As the state has taken over many of the welfare and educational functions formerly provided by religious organizations, these organizations may well have lost some of their capacity to solicit participation. Whether this possibility seems likely depends, of course, on the conception of religion that one adopts. If religion is seen strictly as a differentiated institution concerned only with the privatized spiritual needs of individuals, no inherent conflict between the welfare state and religious organizations is likely to be posited. But if religious organizations are understood as multifunctional associations that not only appeal to spiritual needs but also supply welfare services and give persons an opportunity to contribute to these services, then some conflict between state expansion and religion seems more likely. In this view, state expansion means that the state increasingly becomes "where the action is," rather than religion. Therefore, if one

---

16. See Hugh Hartshorne, Helen R. Stearns, and Willard E. Uphaus, *Standards and Trends in Religious Education* (New Haven: Yale University Press, 1933).

17. See H. Paul Douglass, *The St. Louis Church Survey* (New York: Doran, 1924).

18. See H. Paul Douglass and Edmund de S. Brunner, *The Protestant Church as a Social Institution* (New York: Russell and Russell, 1935), p. 192.

wishes to exercise power or engage in activities that make a difference to the society, one engages in activities related specifically to the state, not in religious activities.

At the same time, all of the arguments that have been mentioned in opposition to the state expansion/civil privatism thesis more generally can also be applied to the context of religious organizations. Some theories of the state specifically refer to religious organizations as one of the kinds of voluntary associations that the state may use to forge its "ruling class coalition." The arguments about voluntary associations being able to bargain for tax breaks, capitalizing on resources supplied by the state, and mobilizing around new definitions of rights and group interests also clearly apply to religious organizations.

It is, therefore, possible to generate arguments both for and against the idea that state expansion may be eroding the strength of religious organizations. In order to decide between these opposing arguments we turn to an examination of some empirical data.

EVIDENCE ON PROTESTANT CHURCH MEMBERSHIP

Religious organizations provide an especially valuable source of data with which to test the foregoing arguments for the following reasons: (1) They are one of the few—perhaps the *only*—type of voluntary association for which comprehensive national membership figures are available at the state level for at least two distinct time periods. (2) Unlike many voluntary associations that exist mainly on paper or at the national level, churches are organized at the *local* level, that is, they are organized into more than 200,000 local congregations (Protestant only) which average approximately 300 members each. (3) In contrast to many voluntary associations, membership in churches is not arbitrarily restricted to persons with particular qualifications; it is instead open to virtually every segment of society, and organizations are available within easy commuting distance of nearly every geographical location. (4) Compared with other kinds of voluntary associations, churches are also one of the most numerous: according to one recent study, the 200,000 Protestant congregations in the United States compare with only 37,000 privately sponsored human service agencies, 14,000 national nonprofit associations, 2,000 cultural organizations, and 3,500 private hospitals.[19] (5) While ex-

19. See Ralph Kramer, *Voluntary Agencies in the Welfare State* (Berkeley and Los Angeles: University of California Press, 1981), p. 1.

pectations vary by denomination, membership in churches generally implies other kinds of voluntary involvement in these organizations as well;
thus, some 40 percent of the adult population in the United States attends religious services for at least an hour in a typical week, and total
giving to religious organizations amounts to more than $22 billion (1980
figures). (6) Because of legal separation of church and state, religious organizations are truly components of the private or voluntary sphere, receiving almost all their support from private sources, whereas nearly half
the support received by "nonprofit organizations" of other kinds is actually supplied by government; in other words, religious memberships
provide a relatively "pure" test of the relation between the state and private voluntary associations.[20]

To be sure, these comparisons also underscore the fact that
religious memberships cannot be taken as representative of all kinds
of voluntary association involvement. Nevertheless, studies of the
correlates of church membership point strongly to the similarities between church membership and involvement in other kinds of less
readily measured voluntary associations or activities. For example,
sample surveys reveal strong correlations between church membership and nonchurch organization memberships, attendance at meetings of nonchurch groups, involvement in volunteer work, and voting
in local elections. Indeed, much of the evidence suggests that church
membership, ironically, is more closely associated with other measures of voluntary participation than it is with different indicators of
religiosity.

The effects of state expansion on religious membership have
not, to my knowledge, been examined previously. Despite the prominence of the state in the more general literature, as well as in specific
discussions of church and state, most interpretations of variations and
trends in church membership have not examined this relation. In addition to the literature already cited, a number of studies have also recently
reopened the question of the state's relation to religion from various
policy perspectives. This gap in the empirical literature is therefore particularly surprising, in view of the number of other analyses that have
been performed at the aggregate level relating religious membership to
various indicators of population, agriculture, manufacturing, geography,
and political orientation.

Church membership data for the 48 contiguous United States
was obtained from surveys in 1952 and 1981 sponsored by the National

20. Ibid., p. 69.

Council of Churches.[21] The 1952 survey included 114 Judeo-Christian denominations and 182,856 congregations, and the 1981 survey included 111 denominations and 231,708 congregations. Both studies provided excellent coverage, with the 1952 survey improving on the 1936 United States Census of Religious Bodies, and the 1981 survey including approximately 91 percent of all church members, although in both studies, black denominations were underrepresented.[22]

The basic definition of church membership used in this study was regular, voluntary members with full membership status, 13 years and older.[23] In 1952, the Catholic churches, Latter-Day Saints (LDS) churches, and Jewish synagogues reported only adherent data (which included prescribed persons and persons of all ages); in 1981, the Catholic and LDS churches again provided only adherent data. Because voluntary ("confirmed") membership data was not available for these denominations, they were excluded from the church membership count; thus, church membership, for present purposes, reflects only Protestant denominations.

Protestant church membership rate was defined as the percentage of the "potential" Protestant membership that were in fact members of a Protestant church. Thus, all persons in a state's population who were either too young to be likely to have joined a Protestant church, or who were already classified as Catholics, Jews, or Mormons, were excluded from consideration. This "base population" was then compared with the number of actual members in Protestant denominations to calculate whether a state scored relatively high or

21. These data are discussed in Lauris B. Whitman and G. W. Trimble, *Churches and Church Membership in the United States, 1951* (Washington, D.C.: Glenmary Research Center, 1954); and Bernard H. Quinn, M. Bradley Anderson, P. Goetting, and P. Shriver, *Churches and Church Membership in the United States, 1981* (Atlanta, GA: Glenmary Research Center, 1984). Although church membership data were available at the county level, we used state as the unit of analysis because (1) county boundaries have changed between the two time periods, while state boundaries have not; (2) data on migration were not available at the county level; and (3) government expenditure, the key independent variable, is primarily generated at the state and federal level.

22. In 1952, none of the predominantly black denominations supplied membership totals, and in 1982, only four predominantly black denominations provided membership totals (African Methodist Episcopal Zion Church, the Bible Church of Christ, the Christian Methodist Episcopal Church, and the Fire Baptized Holiness Church [Wesleyan]). To ensure commensurability across years, these four denominations were omitted from the 1981 data and adjusted both years for the absence of black denominations.

23. For those denominations that did not use 13 as a minimum age for membership, the membership figure was multiplied by the ratio of the 13+ state population to the minimum-age-and-over state population.

low compared with the numbers of people who might have been church members. It might be noted that this rate had declined significantly between the two periods: from a state-level average of 42.1 to 36.1 percent of the population between 1952 and 1981. Indeed, all but five states showed a decrease in percent membership (the exceptions were Mississippi, Alabama, Arkansas, Nebraska, and Oklahoma). In absolute terms, this decline represents a net "loss" of approximately nine million members.

As suggested above, the expansion of government provides a potential explanation for this broad decline in church membership rates. A good measure of government expansion is the money that government spends, that is, total government expenditure per capita.[24] For present purposes, government expenditure was defined as all money spent by the state and the federal government at the state level, as well as all money spent by local and county governments aggregated to the state level. These expenditures do, in fact, parallel the dramatic growth in government activity in recent decades. Average spending per capita at the state level almost tripled between 1952 and 1981, with *every* state showing at least a doubling in the period.

In examining the relationship between Protestant church membership rates and government expenditure, a number of other factors that were expected to affect church membership were included. For example, the percent of the population in each state that was Catholic was included for the following reason: if Catholic churches are perceived by Protestant churches as competing for members and affiliates from among the unaffiliated population, a relatively large Catholic population could stimulate Protestant recruitment efforts. In addition, urban residents have been found to be less likely to be church members than rural residents, presumably as a result of the atomizing aspects of urban life. Similarly, persons who have moved in the past year tend to have weaker ties to their new community and therefore join churches less frequently than do their less mobile counterparts. We took account of these two effects by controlling for the percent of the state's population that lived in urban areas and the percent of households that had moved in a one-year period.

Briefly, the results of the analysis were as follows: There was

---

24. As total government expenditure per capita and social spending (health, education, and welfare) per capita are so highly correlated for each year (1952: $r = .86$; 1981: $r = .83$; both $p < .001$), we analyzed the former measure of expansion because it better reflects the growing role of government in *all* aspects of daily life.

a negative relationship between Protestant church membership rates and government expenditures in both the 1952 data and the data for the two time periods combined. In other words, states that had higher levels of government expenditures had lower levels of Protestant church membership; and states with low government expenditures had higher rates of church membership. These patterns held up when the other factors that might have influenced church membership were taken into account. In addition, some of these other factors also had interesting effects on church membership rates. Urbanization seemed to have a consistent negative effect; that is, states with high percentages of their populations living in urban areas were states with lower levels of Protestant membership. Catholics as a proportion of the population had a positive effect on church membership in 1952, but this effect was not at all significant in the combined data. Surprisingly, migration was clearly not significant, throwing into doubt the relationship between migration and church membership.

GOVERNMENT ACTIVITY AND THE CHURCHES

These results lend some support to the idea that state expansion is associated with civil privatism, at least for the churches. Variation in government expenditure across states was apparently negatively associated with membership in Protestant churches in both the 1952 and 1952/1981 pooled data, controlling for effects of urbanization, residential mobility, region, and the proportion of the state's populations that were Catholic or black.

These patterns need to be put into context. Religious organizations, however broad their activities, are not oriented primarily toward the state. Many of their activities are concerned with needs and interests that the state makes no effort to address at all. Moreover, churches have a well-established organizational base with a long institutional history. For this reason, they should be less susceptible to changes in environmental circumstances. In short, religious organizations would on the surface appear to be relatively immune to negative repercussions from state expansion.

The absolute strength of religious organizations in the United States has, in fact, remained quite high over the past quarter of a century; certainly its present strength, if diminished in some denominations, is on the whole higher than in any other industrialized country. Nevertheless, state expansion does appear to have had a negative effect on voluntary membership in religious organizations. In view of the reasons to have expected otherwise, this fact appears all the more significant.

At the same time, other kinds of voluntary associations may well be in a better position to withstand the corrosive effects of state expansion than religious organizations. To the extent that the society has become more complex and political issues more focused, it may be that voluntary associations with greater degrees of specialization than religious organizations are better able to adapt to state expansion. The tremendous growth of special interest groups in recent years attests to this possibility.

Insofar as the state has actually developed collaborative relations with some types of voluntary agencies, religious organizations may also be in a relatively unfavorable position because of constitutional restrictions separating church and state. It has also been suggested that the state's role in generating resources, such as education and enlarged consumer markets, or in defining rights and entitlements, has favored the growth of some kinds of voluntary associations at the expense of what may be regarded as the more traditional functions of religious organizations. Thus, numbers of national nonprofit associations of other kinds have generally shown significant increases over the past several decades at the same time that voluntary membership in religious organizations has decreased.

It is, therefore, well to adopt a balanced perspective on the role of the modern welfare state in conjunction with arguments about civil privatism. Radical doomsayers who foresee nothing but an atomized populace devoid of all associational attachments clearly overstate their case, as the counterarguments that have been considered here suggest. Yet the effects of state expansion must also be recognized. Even in an institutional area seemingly as well differentiated from the state as religion, state expansion appears to have a significant effect that could, unless counterbalanced by other tendencies, result in an increase of civil privatism.

Six   Paradox and Media

FEW DEVELOPMENTS IN AMERICAN RELIGION illustrate so effectively the
impact of government expansion, technology, and higher education
on matters of faith as the rise of religious television. Bred of favorable
changes in FCC regulations, succored by the latest advances in
telecommunications technology, and deeply conditioned by the rising
influence of higher education, religious television provides a vivid example of the social processes that have transformed American religion
in recent decades.

Religion is a way of coping with the pathos and paradox of
our lives. But when religion is beamed into our living rooms from
sleek, high-technology studios via satellite hookups, it creates its own
pathos and becomes the source of paradox itself. The pathos is obvious enough. The paradox requires closer attention, as paradoxes always do.

To many, the advent and rapid growth of religious television
exemplifies the continuing vitality of evangelical religion in American
society. Therefore, to suggest that religious television may instead be
linked to some of the most thoroughly secularized forces currently
operating is likely to seem either farfetched or hopelessly naive. Nevertheless, it is this relationship that deserves attention, not in order to
cast any doubt on the sincerity of the televangelists or their audiences,
but as a means of illuminating the deep extent to which social condi-

tions have influenced the character of American religion. Framed in perhaps a less provocative way, the question at issue is not one of scrutinizing the message of the television preachers for some hidden agenda—as many in the theological establishment have been prone to do—but of utilizing the development of religious television as a case in point for examining some popular conceptions about the dynamics of the secular in our society.

THE PRIVATIZATION OF AMERICAN FAITH?

One of the most frequently advanced characterizations of American religion is that it is becoming increasingly "privatized." That is, the public, corporate, communal quality of religion is said to be declining, leaving individuals with their own highly subjective and idiosyncratic expressions of faith. The terms "private" or "privatized" actually carry several connotations in this context.

One connotation suggests that the religion practiced by an increasing number of Americans may be entirely of their own manufacture—a kind of eclectic synthesis of Christianity, popular psychology, *Reader's Digest* folklore, and personal superstitions, all wrapped up in the anecdotes of the individual's biography.

A different connotation suggests that religious practices remain subject to much more orthodox influences, namely, the churches and synagogues; they have no influence on public affairs in the world of business and politics. According to this conception, religion has withdrawn into the "private sphere" to function much in the same manner as leisure activities, voluntary gatherings, and family relations.

Still another connotation focuses on the possibility that even within the private sector religious expression may have become less public, less organized, less relational, leaving individuals radically alone in their experience of the divine. All three of these connotations bear some resemblance to popular images of American religion.

The idea that religious expression is becoming increasingly the product of individual biographies is supported by the very fact of America's pluralistic religious culture. With several hundred different denominations, sects, and cults to choose from, every individual can pretty much tailor his or her religious views to personal taste. As individuals are increasingly exposed to the teachings of different faiths through books, television, travel, and geographic mobility, eclecticism becomes the likely result. This tendency is also reinforced by the highly individualistic ethos in American culture which asserts the individual's freedom of conscience in matters of religion. We believe that individuals should make up their own minds about what they believe, drawing on whatever sources of inspiration they may find. Thus, it is not uncommon to find public expressions—President Eisenhower's famous remark uttered in the 1950s, for example—that faith is important, but we do not care what that faith is.

The second meaning of privatization—that religion has no influence in the public sphere—seems on the surface to be contradicted by the voracious appetite that American politics has shown for religious influences. From the civil rights movement to the anti-abortion campaign, examples of religion playing a direct role in public affairs are scarcely difficult to identify. Yet these examples fail to contradict the deeper insights of this version of the privatization argument. The question is not so much whether clergy lead sit-ins or presidents draw support from religious groups, but whether any of these activities matters on as broad a scale as it once did.

The argument of theorists who have advanced the idea of privatization is that a greater and greater share of the decisions affecting public life are made strictly on grounds of economic profitability, technical feasibility, and political control. Indeed, even this formulation may be an understatement, since it suggests greater exercise of conscious decision-making capacities than may be the case, given the tremendous complexity of economic forces, bureaucracies, and vested interests that shape social life. For the individual the effect of these impersonal forces is seen increasingly in a withdrawal from active participation in political life (other than voting), in evidence of psychological alienation from government and business, and in actual retreat into the private pleasures of consumerism, personal hobbies, and the nuclear isolated family.

Religion, social theorists claim, has accommodated itself to this broader retreat from public life. Apart from obvious exceptions such as religious organizations against nuclear warfare or abortion, the evidence suggests that churches focus the bulk of their resources in areas dealing with personal spirituality, moral behavior, childrearing, marital relations, and emotional care, rather than delving into the implications of religious values for issues of community planning, capital investment, business conduct, social justice, or public policy.

Many religious leaders will, of course, defend these preferences on grounds of scriptural or theological insight as well as pragmatic considerations of church unity and growth. Nevertheless, the removal of religious priorities from the public sphere merely supports the allegation that it is becoming more deeply privatized.

The third connotation of privatization—that even within the religious sphere communal ties are breaking down—draws support from arguments about the increasing anonymity and isolation of modern society in general. The terms in which this discussion has been cast are household phrases—"lonely crowd," "mass society," "secular city." As cities have grown, as geographic mobility has increased, as small neighborhoods and villages have been replaced with shopping malls and football stadia, this argument suggests, fewer and fewer people participate intimately in primary support groups. Instead, they exist as nameless faces in the crowd, associating mainly with strangers with whom they have only fleeting and highly instrumental relations.

The religious realm may offer one of the few refuges from this anonymous existence, providing opportunities for fellowship, sharing of common interests, and firsthand relations free of instrumental calculations. Yet the question has been raised whether these activities may also be eroding in the face of broader societal tendencies. If, for example, the typical American moves at least once every five years, can religious groups provide the kind of intimate fellowship that may have once existed in rural or small-town churches with more stable memberships? If the typical church finds it necessary to hold worship services for 500 to 1,000 members in order to achieve competitive economies of scale, do religious communities eventually come to resemble audiences and spectator sports rather than supportive groups?

The widening appeal of religious television adds new considerations to the discussion of privatization in all three of its current usages. Does it lead to greater eclecticism in individual religious styles? Does it reinforce the tendency for religion to become a purely private leisure-time activity? And does it further weaken the relational bonds of religious communities?

To see how these questions work out in practice, let us consider a typical (but hypothetical) case: the case of Mrs. Miller, or Mabel, as her hypothetical friends call her. Mabel has tuned in the Jimmy Swaggart show on more than one occasion—at least she used to before Jimmy's sins became public. She also watched Jim Bakker's "PTL Club"—that is, before Jim and Tammy fell from grace. And from time to time she picked up the "700 Club" on one of her cable channels, although she missed Pat Robertson during his bid for political power.

On the whole, things have not been going so well for Mabel's religious television heroes. But still, she has no trouble finding preachers with a flair for the fiery pulpit rhetoric she loves and the reassuring devotional messages that warm her heart: Jerry Falwell and Robert Schuller and Rex Humbard and others.

This particular day happens to be a Sunday, and as she has done on Sunday mornings for nearly 65 years, Mabel rises early. As a child growing up in Iowa, she used to be awakened promptly at 7 o'clock on Sunday mornings so her mother could braid her hair and make sure everyone had a hearty breakfast in time to get to Sunday school by 9:45. That was always the appointed hour at the little Baptist church seven miles down the road. Later on, it was Mabel's turn to rise in time to get her own children dressed for Sunday school, and in time to get the pot roast in the oven and the table set for the Sunday feast. In recent years, Mabel has been alone, but the habit of early rising persists. And so, as she sits down to breakfast, she flips on the television and automatically passes by the morning cartoons, the old movies, the local version of Oprah Winfrey, and the weather channel, and settles into an hour of inspiration and revival.

Now Mabel, as I said, is a typical viewer. She does not watch television preaching every afternoon and evening, and sometimes she does not even feel like watching on Sunday mornings. But like about one-third of the U.S. population, she has watched at least one religious program on television in the past month.[1] Were the omnipresent Gallup pollster to come to her door this morning, Mabel's responses would not surprise him.

She likes to watch Jimmy Swaggart and the others, she says, because of the music and the preaching. She feels close to God when she does. The music lifts her spirits. The preaching challenges her to be a better Christian. And somehow, she just feels good about watching. In fact, she sometimes feels more inspired than she does at the Baptist church (still down the road), and she even sent in a check once when Jimmy seemed to be in really desperate straits.

So there she is: Mabel alone in her living room getting God via satellite. She epitomizes what sociologists have been calling

---

1. This figure and the social characteristics of viewers discussed in the following paragraphs are based on findings from a national survey conducted by the Gallup Organization in 1984 as part of a major study of religious television; see G. L. Gerbner, S. Hoover, M. Morgan, N. Signorilli, H. Cotugno, and R. Wuthnow, *Religion and Television: A Research Report by the Annenberg School of Communications, University of Pennsylvania, and the Gallup Organization, Inc.* (Philadelphia: The Annenberg School of Communications, 1984); for additional analyses of these data and commentary, see the articles in *Review of Religious Research* 29 (December 1987): 97-210.

privatized religion.[2] She is no longer active in the Ladies' Missionary Society, she is a thousand miles from her nearest of kin, cut off from the real world except for the few friends she plays canasta with on Thursday afternoons. Now she does not even need to venture down the road to the Baptist church to fulfill her religious needs. Next she will have abandoned her religious community entirely and developed her own unique version of personalized religiosity—"Mabelism," she will probably call it.

Sociologists would argue that Mabel is caught up in the powerful vortex of a downward social spiral. It is not exactly her fault that her faith has become privatized. Even when her mother was rousting her out of bed as a little girl, the Baptist church was becoming more privatized simply by virtue of having to compete with two hundred other denominations, no one of which could speak authoritatively about the word of God. In the intervening decades, privatization was also reinforced by the growth of anonymous urban places, by the shattering of local kin networks as college training required children to move away and then as professional occupations required them to stay away. In all of this, a kind of rugged frontier spirit animated everyone's sense of his or her individual uniqueness.

In addition, one could not help having been shaped by all those commercials that said you could have your hamburgers done "your way," by all those car salesmen that encouraged you to have your Chevrolet customized to your own specifications, and by all those *Reader's Digest* articles about brave soldiers and eccentric millionaires who succeeded by bucking the system.

But televised preaching seemed to be the final stroke. If anything should draw people out of the secret recesses of their homes and force them to live "in community," it was the church. The Bible itself commanded believers not to forsake the assemblying of themselves together. It was in the midst of the assembled faithful that the miracle of *kerygma* happened. Now television was replacing this community with a miracle of its own—the miracle of sitting motionless and alone before a preacher thousands of miles away who could not listen, who could not love, but could only speak.

Of course, this depiction of religious television is—in the hypothetical way I have presented it—a caricature. Nevertheless, it is a very familiar and disturbing image of the fruits of religious television.

2. See especially Thomas Luckmann, *The Invisible Religion: The Problem of Religion in Modern Society* (New York: Macmillan, 1967).

It lies behind the anxious questions one hears from clergy about religious television; it reinforces the cynicism that college students always express toward television preaching; and it has funneled hundreds of thousands of dollars—yes, into the hands of television preachers—but also into the budgets of research institutes and polling agencies. It is a caricature that contains a great deal of truth, and yet one that neglects an extremely important dimension of religious television.

Let us return momentarily to our hypothetical case. Mabel does sit alone in her living room watching her favorite television preachers. But the spectacle she views is also very much a part of our public religion—for good or for bad. The Jim Bakker and Jimmy Swaggart sex scandals prompted widely publicized discussions of the nature of morality and its relation to public religious figures. Pat Robertson's abortive presidential candidacy generated hopes and fears about the mixing of religion and politics. Jerry Falwell has used the money his viewers send in to launch a vast movement to restore morality to American public life. Robert Schuller routinely gives his pulpit to guest speakers from Washington who tell how important their faith is to their functioning as public officials.

Where is Mabel in all of this? Simply a passive spectator like one of the nameless faces in the crowd who looked on as Hitler rose to power? She might be. But let us pursue her interview with our imaginary Gallup pollster a bit further. Why does she watch?

Her concerns, it turns out, are not so strictly private as we thought. She tells of her deep interest in the direction moral standards have been going in recent years. She watches, she says, to gain information about important social and political issues of the day. She routinely receives letters from Jerry Falwell, sometimes sent by certified mail, which keep her abreast of the latest developments at the Supreme Court and in the White House.

Once, shortly after she had mailed her second check to Lynchburg, she even received a phone call asking if she could sign a petition and send another check to help fight a worthy cause. She has also noticed in recent weeks that she is getting newsletters from Senator Jesse Helms, the National Rifle Association, and from a former Air Force general who is running an organization called "High Frontier." Mabel feels more connected to national politics than she has ever felt in her life.

What do we infer? Certainly the development of televised religion has done more than simply contribute to the privatization of faith. It has also reinforced the role of religion in the public sphere. It generates huge sums of money from which political candidacies can be launched. It provides new ways for individual citizens like Mabel to express their sentiments and see them mobilized along with the sentiments of millions of others.

Jimmy Swaggart is a public figure no less than Ronald Reagan or Citizen Kane. Both his faults and his rhetoric place religion on the national agenda. He has done for our generation what Theodore Weld or Billy Sunday or Aimee Semple McPherson did for previous generations: he has made religion something people talk about, an item of public debate. The secularists may well have the final say, but they find themselves having to confront religion all over again—and long after they thought they had simply pushed religion into the dark crevices of our private lives.

So the paradox of televised religion is this: at the same time it privatizes, it also makes public. At one level this conclusion should not surprise us. Only the theoretical blinders that have guided the social scientist in probing this issue have prevented us from recognizing, as Mabel Miller herself probably would, that religious television is both private and public. But having made this simple observation, we are now in a position to press the matter onto somewhat less charted terrain. I want, in particular, to consider two important questions: How private (really) is the private side of religious television; or, conversely, how public is its public side? Do the private and the public here simply stand side by side or do they—in some curious way—reinforce one another?

HOW PRIVATE IS THE PRIVATE?

The reason this question is important is that an awful lot of the argument about religious television and privatization has been stacked up on the precarious fact that Mabel sits alone in her living room when she watches. Indeed, she probably does. But how private is this behavior (really) and what should it be compared to?

From our not-so-imaginary Gallup pollsters we know three things about Mabel's viewing behavior that should cause us to pull up a bit short. First, the typical Mabel discusses what she watches with friends, family, and fellow churchgoers. In other words, the proverbial "two-step" model of communication is at work here. Jerry Falwell makes his pitch via the airwaves. But what Mabel and her friends hear—and how they respond—is filtered through the networks of direct social interaction. Mabel may watch alone, but she knows others are watching, she knows others who are watching, and they form an important part of her actual community. Second, unlike Mabel herself, who because she lives alone also watches alone, a large minority of religious television viewers watch with someone else present. Their viewing may still be very much private, but with someone else present their chances of discussing what they see become infinitely increased. Third, the typical Mabel who watches sporadically—and even the atypical Mabel who is hooked on religious television—remains just as likely as anyone else having the same religious beliefs and social characteristics to attend church in person and to donate money to religious organizations unrelated to television.

Part of what has led our thinking astray seems to be that much of what religious broadcasters put on television consists of sermons and worship services taped in real congregations. For this reason, we have assumed that people who watched these services must be doing so instead of actually attending them in person. But we now know differently—because of what our survey studies have shown us. These studies also tell us why people who watch religious television do not give up participating in religious services personally. Heavy viewers are also extremely devout: they just cannot get enough religion, it seems. They also receive different sorts of gratifications from the two: from television they gain inspiration and a sense of knowing what's going on; from personal participation, a sense of worship and feeling close to God and other people. Both are important.

Apart from such research findings, we can also be instructed by letting ourselves imagine for a moment the kinds of religious activities the devout have engaged in through the long centuries before television was invented. They went to church, of course, and they probably turned out in those proverbial frontier towns to witness the traveling revivalist preach hellfire to the community and conduct mass baptisms. At least this is the image we have had conjured up for us by sociologists who have likened the contemporary televangelists to the itinerant tent-meeting revivalists of the past. The devout did some other things, though: they prayed and they read their Bibles; they held family devotions with their children, said grace at meals, studied their Sunday school lessons, learned catechism questions, whistled hymns while they washed the dishes or tilled the fields, read the penny leaflets inserted in their church bulletins, and if they were serious enough about it bought tracts and inspirational books and consumed them in their free moments. In short, religion has always had its private dimensions.

Religion television, therefore, needs to be considered in the proper perspective. What people see on television may be similar rhetorically to the hysteria of mass revivals. But it may also be similar rhetorically to the devotional guides they used to meditate on privately. And its purpose may be less to replace public religious gatherings than to add another dimension to the life of religious devotion and experience. This seems to be part of the answer to my question about how private religious television really is.

Another important part of the answer requires us to focus for a moment on the differences and similarities between two kinds of religious services: the ones we attend personally and the ones we view on television. In one sense, of course, the viewer is at an enormous disadvantage compared with the person who actually attends. Sitting there on her sofa, Mabel can hardly experience the vibrancy of singing along with two or three hundred other voices. She misses the opportunity to exchange greetings with friends and neighbors after the service is over. She is not as likely to feel that special twinge of conscience when the preacher looks her directly in the eye. And she cannot tell the preacher how she felt about what he said as she goes out the door.

All of that is obvious, but we should not ignore the limitations one faces in attending a religious service in person either. Suppose Mabel arrives a bit late and has to sit way in the back or behind the pillar. Suppose she has grown a little hard of hearing and has trouble making out what the preacher said. Suppose she has only recently moved to this community or has been too much in ill health during the winter months to attend regularly. Nothing can be more alienating than sitting amidst a crowd of people and yet being a stranger in their midst. Or, quite aside from any of these impediments, suppose Mabel is just a parishioner in good standing who sits up front and pays close attention to the preacher. Is she free to look about, to stare at the people behind her, to scan their faces to see if they are responding the same way she is? Is her consciousness really dominated by the collectivity? Or is it likely to be dominated by the single voice that dominates her vision and her hearing?

We have only to watch religious services on television with these questions in mind to recognize some of the advantages of being a viewer. Our eye is not at liberty to stay glued either to the face in the pulpit or on the Bible in our lap. The camera forces our eye to follow it. First we glimpse the choir as a whole in all its splendor, then we zero in on one choir member after another, gaining a sense of their individuality but also of the fact that each one contributes to the overall harmony. We focus for a moment on the pastor's face as he begins to preach, but then a wider angle shows us that he is flanked by more than a dozen important-looking men in business suits. He speaks for them, too, we must conclude, and they are there (literally) to back him up. Then, as Robert Schuller's rhetoric goes on, the camera scans the Crystal Cathedral in all its majesty. We are impressed by the enormity of the building and by the magnitude of the audience assembled within it. Suddenly we feel we are part of something very large, very important. The camera soars up to the crystal ceiling and then around the grounds, showing us the beauties of a southern California sky, flowers in bloom, waterfalls, birds. And, with different nuances, we experience the same mixture of divine and earthly splendor as the camera takes us vicariously to Jimmy Swaggart's Family Worship Center in Baton Rouge or to Jerry Falwell's Thomas Road Church in Lynchburg.

All of this trains our eye in a way that makes it impossible for us to escape the communal dimension of the worship service. Then, as if to overcome the danger of letting us feel for a moment that we are outsiders, the camera also provides us with visual models with which we can identify. As the audience laughs the camera shows a close-up of a handsome middle-aged man enjoying the joke: he shows us how to enjoy it too. Turn in your Bibles to verse 36, the preacher asserts, and we see a black teenager in the audience dutifully performing the act. Won't you repent and accept Jesus into your heart, he intones, and our own fleeting sense of guilt and response is magnified by the anguish we see on the face of an elderly woman with wizened flesh.

The point I hope these examples make clear is that no simple correlation can be suggested between the rise of religious television and the privatization of faith. Religious television certainly has a private dimension, but so does any kind of religion—we would not regard it a very profound sort of faith that did not. It may be useful, as I have suggested, to liken religious television to the devotional dimension of traditional religion. Rather than asking how religious television viewing differs from attending religious services in person, therefore, we might want to focus attention on the contrasts and similarities between religious television viewing and such long-standing devotional practices as Bible reading, prayer, and meditation.

THE PUBLIC DIMENSION

At the same time, my examples underscore the fact that religious television has a public dimension. Televangelists have become stars of the public media, as nearly any week spent viewing the Johnny Carson show, "Saturday Night Live," or the Donahue program will reveal. Their organizations are massive social institutions, no less than any church or denomination is a social institution. And the issues they have raised — political conservatism, rights of the unborn, capital punishment, preachers in politics, world hunger, conflicts in the Middle East, the social propriety of homosexuality, just to name a few — include a great number of questions about where the nation as a whole should be headed and how the public, as public, should think about these directions.

We are likely to get farther, therefore, by considering both the private and the public dimensions of religious television, rather than simply asking whether religious television has tipped the overall balance somehow toward the private at the expense of the public. I would like to focus on several problematic aspects of the private and public dimensions of religious television.

ACTIVE INVOLVEMENT IN ONE'S FAITH

To what degree does religious television encourage active, spontaneous involvement on the part of the individual in the construction of his or her religious expressions, as opposed to a more passive and externally guided form of religious expression?

If we think for a moment about devotional religion in general, we immediately recognize wide variation in the extent to which active and spontaneous involvement is encouraged. In many liturgical traditions, for example, the individual believer is encouraged to participate actively in personal and group prayer, or in the sacraments, but only to the extent of mouthing what is recommended in a standard guide, such as a book of common prayer or a printed order of service in the weekly church leaflet. In contrast, many other traditions encourage the individual believer to make up his or her own prayers, to use new words, and to tailor them to his or her immediate situation. Some traditions go farther still, encouraging the believer to take the initiative to engage in individual Bible study, or to keep a daily diary of one's thoughts about God, or to seek out ways in one's daily life to witness or give testimony to one's faith.

It is often difficult, of course, to know whether the individual is genuinely acting from spontaneous internal impulses or whether the individual is really conforming to some external set of expectations. The motivation behind such actions is not the issue, however; nor does it necessarily run counter to active, spontaneous forms of religious expression to follow various role models or scripts that one has observed. The important differences remain, at least at the two extremes.

At one extreme, the individual sits passively and does little else but listen: someone reads the Scriptures to him, prays for him, and presents him with music to listen to; his attention is guided from one activity to another; he therefore has little opportunity to make choices about when and how to respond or participate; even the opportunities he is given to respond may be highly structured. At the other extreme, the individual moves and speaks and does so with some element of spontaneity: he may go on a religious pilgrimage or at least go to a specially designated place of worship; he reads for himself and sings for himself; he is suddenly flooded with ecstasy to the point that he can no longer read or sing and has to pause momentarily to soak up the moment and give thanks for it; or he finds himself utterly bored and emotionless so he decides to abandon the devotional book he was reading and pick up something else instead.

It should be clear from these examples that religious television viewing falls more toward the passive end of the scale. The viewer sits quietly and listens to what the talk show host or televangelist has to say. He has only to listen as the Scripture verses for the day are read to him. Rather than picking up his own Bible and finding the passage for himself, he watches as a teleprompter shows him the words on the screen. He listens as the choir sings instead of rising to his feet and singing along. Even his responses are modeled for him: after the televangelist says something humorous, the camera zeroes in on the face of someone in the crowd who especially enjoyed the joke; when the choir raises its voice in a crescendo of praise for the beauties of nature, the camera zeroes in on the bouquet before the altar or takes one on a quick, visually uplifting tour of beautifully landscaped grounds. When it comes time to receive the offering, an 800-number flashes on the screen and the quiet voice, not of one's conscience, but of the announcer, suggests that a pledge of $100 would be appropriate for today.

The couch potato image of the habitual television viewer comes inescapably to mind. Of course, one can spontaneously register one's boredom with the screen by flipping channels or even by turning off the set entirely. One can also become more actively involved in the devotional reflections stimulated by the program; for example, by writing to the televangelist for his latest book, by reading carefully the direct-mail solicitations he sends to your house, or by turning one's VCR to "hold" and spending a few moments in private prayer. The religious television programmers do not encourage most of these spontaneous actions, however. Their work succeeds best when they can program millions of viewers to watch at the same time every week, to sit passively and listen (even, one sometimes wonders, to listen at more of a subliminal level than to listen critically), and to send in one's check dutifully for the amount prescribed.

On this criterion, then, the role of religious television is not so much to privatize faith as to render it passive. One might even argue that the individual who actively and spontaneously works out his own way of responding to God has a more privatized faith than the person who simply responds in the way that millions of other viewers respond. A passive faith is private only in the additional sense that if one never speaks, never behaves, and never ventures beyond the confines of one's living room, then nobody else is ever likely to know of one's faith commitments. Prayer has truly remained in the closet and one's light has stayed hidden beneath a bushel basket.

Of course, one cannot credit these faults entirely to the advent of religious television. The institutional church has always had a stake in promoting passivity about many aspects of the faith. Just as the televangelists hope their viewers will sit quietly and listen, so the preachers who fill live pulpits generally find their burdens easier if their parishioners sit quietly and listen, responding only when the choirmaster directs or when the plate is passed. Any orderly worship service requires it, although the anomaly between such passivity and a genuine spirit of worship is often striking. Annie Dillard has captured well this ironic sense of anomaly. "Does anyone," she writes, "have the foggiest idea what sort of power we so blithely invoke?"

> The churches are children playing on the floor with their chemistry sets, mixing up a batch of TNT to kill a Sunday morning. It is madness to wear ladies' straw hats and velvet hats to church; we should all be wearing crash helmets. Ushers should issue life preservers and signal flares; they should lash us to our pews. For the sleeping god may wake someday and take offense, or the waking god may draw us out to where we can never return.[3]

But even more private expressions of religious devotion, where greater variation might be tolerated, seem to confront a con-

---

3. Annie Dillard, *Teaching a Stone to Talk: Expeditions and Encounters* (New York: Harper & Row, 1982), pp. 40-41.

stant tension between activity and passivity, spontaneity and conformity. Daily prayer books and meditation guides encourage routine in order to make sure the believer does something: rise at the same hour each day, pray at the same time, read a one-page devotional from the guide provided for that month. But do so actively as well: think through one's own religious needs, keep a journal of one's faith journey, and if one feels an urge to burst forth in praise, let it rip!

As with most aspects of the religious life, the question of passivity and activity is one of finding an appropriate balance. Religious television appears to tip the scale far in the direction of passivity, and thus gives rise for concerns about what kinds of more active devotional expressions should be encouraged. But some element of passive, externally guided behavior seems inescapable.

RELIGIOUS TELEVISION AND THE IMAGINATION

To what degree does religious television encourage imagination in the expression of faith, as opposed to a more conformist or doctrinaire style of faith?

This question is closely associated with the previous one: if a form of religious expression encourages passivity, we would also expect it to result in a more conformist or doctrinaire style of faith. My purpose in separating the two issues, though, is to provide an occasion for discussing the ways in which the media of communication themselves may promote or inhibit the religious imagination. To do so, we need to depart momentarily from specific considerations about religious television and consider the effects of televised media more generally in comparison with two other media: live productions and the printed word.

Let us recall briefly two historic episodes in the transition from live productions to the printed word. One occurred in the sixteenth century in conjunction with the Reformation's emphasis on the printed word in opposition to the iconography and festivals of the medieval church. The other came in the eighteenth century during the Enlightenment with the transition in elite culture from the stage to the novel.

In both cases it was argued—by many contemporaries as well as by historians—that the printed word was superior to the live productions that it superseded. In the sixteenth-century case, the arguments focused on the tendency for believers to concretize iconography and festivals, thereby confusing the images for the divine truths they represented. The Reformers railed against the idolatry of graphic images and live productions of all kinds, preferring to limit the believer's sensory stimuli to that of the read and spoken Bible. In the eighteenth-century case, the arguments focused more squarely on the limitations of the drama as genre vis-à-vis the novel. Stage productions were limited in the overall number of scenes they could depict, in the number and relations among characters that audiences could be expected to follow, and in the voice and sense of time that characters could adopt. The novel was said to be more adaptable to the complex plots, situations, and relationships of modern urban life.

Interestingly enough, both arguments bear directly on the relation between the printed word and the imagination. The relation suggested is a curious one—at least in the sense that it runs counter to many of our contemporary theories of the printed word. These theories suggest that the printed word, by virtue of codifying and formalizing discourse, tends to limit meaning. That is, printed discourse spells things out so that there can be no question of what was meant; in contrast, icons, festivals, and stage plays leave more to the imagination.[4] But the arguments in relation to these two historic episodes run just the opposite. They suggest that the printed word leaves more to the imagination.

In the Reformation case, the printed word requires the believer to develop his or her own abstract sense of the divine, rather than having the divine concretized in a visual image. In the Enlightenment case, the printed word requires the reader of, say, *Moll Flanders* to imagine what Moll must have looked like, how her various lovers may have been dressed, and how houses, rooms, and streets all may have met the eye. People apparently found the printed word more appealing precisely because it did not serve everything up on a prearranged platter.

Whether these arguments are valid is for literary historians to debate. But they suggest an interesting parallel for assessing the implications of religious television. Conventional wisdom might again suggest that television enriches the imagination. How much more vivid it is to see the movie rather than to read the book! Similarly, how much more effective it is to be able to see Robert Schuller on

---

4. Relevant arguments can be found in Jerome S. Bruner, Rose R. Oliver, and Patricia M. Greenfield, *Studies in Cognitive Growth* (New York: Wiley, 1966); Basil Bernstein, *Class, Codes and Control* (New York: Schocken, 1975); and Robert N. Bellah, *Beyond Belief: Essays on Religion in a Post-Traditional World* (New York: Harper & Row, 1970).

the screen and to have the camera scan the splendors of the Crystal Cathedral than to have to make do for one's religious devotions a dry half-hour spent reading the book of Romans. If the historic arguments apply, though, religious television stifles the imagination rather than facilitates it.

The reason for this conclusion is that religious television frames the visual stimulus we receive and forces us to focus exclusively on that stimulus. The Crystal Cathedral becomes an icon, and our relation to this icon becomes even less imaginative than it might be if we visited Anaheim in person, because the camera prompts us to focus for ten seconds here and ten seconds there. Our attention must follow the camera's eye. It is also limited by the frame of the picture we see on our screens, quite unlike the subliminal impressions we might obtain from being there and letting peripheral vision play a role.

Similarly, the face of Jerry Falwell becomes an icon that limits our attention, perhaps even to a greater degree when we see it on television than would be the case with our own minister preaching to us directly. The camera zeroes in on Falwell's face; we see every feature; and we see only those expressions the film editors want us to see; whereas our own minister's face on Sunday morning, seen from 50 or 100 feet back, constitutes a much smaller proportion of our overall vision, and we see him or her in unguarded moments that may convey some humanness, rather than the carefully edited incarnation we see on our television screens.

What tempers all of this, I should note, is that much of the programming we see on religious television consists of the spoken word. It is, in that sense, not unlike listening to a tape or even reading one of Robert Schuller's books. Religious television has for the most part avoided featuring graphic images, such as pictures of Jesus, and it has relied only to a small extent (probably because of costs) on televised drama, situation comedies, and documentaries. When Jerry Falwell tells us about the scourge of immorality that is marching at this very hour on our nation's capital, we still have ample room to use our imaginations.

Nevertheless, we have cause to wonder whether religious television stifles the religious imagination. Whether the spoken word predominates in films of church services or in talk show formats, we are still subjected to a great deal of visual imagery. The words we hear Jerry Falwell say are limited in their connotations by the way he says them, but also by our images of the people in his audience, the choir behind him, and the candid conversational shots in his office. Similarly, the words we hear Pat Robertson utter on the "700 Club" are inextricably interwoven with images of the famous Robertson grin, the carefully groomed co-hosts, and the polished stage settings.

The contrast between the religious devotion that comes from these highly structured settings and the lonely prophet in the wilderness contemplating the mysteries of the Great Commandment is profound. So is the contrast between the person whose vision is filled with images of the Thomas Road Church and the child who hears the 23rd Psalm read during family devotions and imagines vividly what the "valley of the shadow of death" must be like.

To return momentarily to the question of privatization, we might ask, Which of these is really the purer form of a privatized religion? Certainly the person who imagines what the Shepherd's Psalm must mean has a more privatized religion, in that instance, than does the person who sees it enacted in a Cecil B. deMille panorama, or even than the person who lets Robert Schuller paint the imagery of what it means. At this level, one would scarcely be inclined to criticize the believer for practicing a privatized form of faith.

THE LIFE OF FAITH—IN COMMUNITY

To what degree does religious television encourage a style of faith that emerges from and is reinforced by social interaction, as opposed to a style of faith that remains more purely the unspoken attribute of the individual?

Some evidence indicates that many viewers of religious television discuss these programs with their families, friends, and fellow churchgoers. In that sense, religious television is not strictly a private matter. One can say to a friend, "What did you think of Jerry Falwell yesterday?" just as easily as one can ask his or her reaction to yesterday's sermon at the local church. Indeed, the odds of any two people having watched the same religious television program may actually be much higher than any two people having attended the same church, in view of the diversity of our society and the demise of the neighborhood church.

Interaction of this kind is likely to reinforce certain beliefs. When one's friend responds, "I thought he really said some important things," your own conviction about Falwell's credibility may rise. Or when you show someone a direct-mail solicitation containing alarming news about how the Soviets are planning to poison our drinking water, and that person registers an appropriate level of concern, your own alarm may well increase. This kind of reinforcement may not be terribly different from that gained at the local church where mutual sharing simply confirms your commitment to the common faith.

In another way, though, the interaction associated with religious television is likely to be quite different from that occurring in a local Bible study or Sunday evening discussion group. The reinforcement one receives about Jerry Falwell's latest sermon is still reinforcement about an authoritative figure. He remains the voice of wisdom, and even if one disagrees, those disagreements never feed back into a genuine discussion. Falwell may castigate his detractors to show what villains they are, but the camera seldom shows him in a roundtable discussion involving genuine give-and-take. The small Bible study or discussion group, at least at its best, can be a source of such give-and-take. One can express a tentative view and have it disputed by another member of the group. One can share a personal anecdote and have it reinforced, but given a slightly different twist, by someone else relating a similar experience. No authority figure dominates. The learning that takes place occurs dialogically, and the group itself provides a model of the mutual respect that lies at the heart of the religious worldview.

One caveat should be mentioned, however. The dialogic experience in which genuine learning takes place may well be absent in primary religious communities, just as it is absent on religious television. Rather than consensus arising out of the group's deliberations, consensus may be so highly valued that no one feels free to share his or her honest opinions. In fact, churches can become models of a tacit consensus that no one dares question. Consequently, serious disagreements never surface; the disgruntled move on to another parish rather than risk unsettling the waters. Polite conversation prevails; sermons focus on "unity" and "brotherhood"; and collective pronouns predominate.

In a pluralistic society, fraught with deeply individualistic values, the virtue of public discussion is to temper purely private sentiments and to let consensus emerge through open dialogue. As I have already suggested, religious television may promote public dialogue at a certain level, but its focus on single authoritative leaders runs counter to the more reciprocal kinds of interchange that can take place at more intimate levels.

PRIVATE INTO PUBLIC

To what degree does religious television integrate concerns from the private realm into public discourse, as opposed to keeping these two spheres separate?

I suggested with my example of Mabel Miller that religious television must be understood as a force in the public sphere, whether or not it also encourages a certain kind of private religion. Of course, one can think of Pat Robertson's presidential candidacy or Jerry Falwell's role in organizing the New Christian Right. These are examples of purely public behavior. But we should also consider the extent to which they infuse the private into the public realm.

Religious television has, although sometimes inadvertently, brought private concerns very much into the public realm. That is, some of the religious sentiments, concerns, and activities that have long been pushed out of the public square have now emerged as items of public display. The most vivid example was Jimmy Swaggart's public confession of his sin with a prostitute.

So unusual was his public display of emotion—tears streaming down his face, voice trembling, begging God's forgiveness—that the mass media were put to some pains to make sense of it all. Some tried to interpret it by placing it in a theatrical frame: Swaggart proved once again what a good actor he is; he really felt nothing but made us think he did. Others placed a medical frame around the episode: Swaggart was just distraught and got over the whole thing quite quickly; or, Swaggart has a mental problem that causes him to do schizophrenic things—he does need rehabilitation. Still others, failing any way to make sense of it at all, poked fun: "The beaches were wild today— beer parties, sex orgies, strip shows," Johnny Carson quipped, "it's time we got those televangelists back to work."

There were perhaps many reasons why the media were unable (or unwilling) to make sense of the Swaggart confession. One reason that must not be overlooked is that repentance and forgiveness are themes that have virtually dropped out of our public culture. We are far more comfortable with retribution, punishment, paying for one's mistakes, lawsuits, vendettas, keeping the record straight, establishing guilt, and fixing the blame than we are with repentance and forgiveness.

Yet repentance and forgiveness are clearly an essential part of the Christian message. Preachers talk about these themes all the time. Jimmy Swaggart made them a public spectacle. Confess one's sins, claim God's forgiveness, and go forward from there. Surely God was good enough to forgive Jimmy Swaggart, and so, by implication, others might be expected to forgive him too. Questions about the public propriety of maintaining a high leadership position were, of course, put aside. But on the surface, the Swaggart scandal functioned as a kind of morality play. Indeed, the Swaggart team was quick to recognize this role. As Swaggart's son Donny articulated it, appealing for viewers' financial support shortly after the episode became public, "If there's no forgiveness for Jimmy Swaggart, there's no forgiveness for you either."

This was an exceptional instance. In other ways, though, religious television has brought a number of previously private issues into the public realm. For example, arguments about abortion, homosexuality, and personal morality have taken issues out of the bedroom and placed them on the national agenda. The televangelists have argued that such matters really cannot be left purely to individual discretion; instead, morality bears on the collective strength of a nation and thus must become an item of political policy and legislation.

In bringing these items into the public sphere, religious television has, one could argue, actually reversed some of the tendency toward privatization that observers have seen in American culture. If Americans have become more and more withdrawn into their own private lives, then turning private concerns into public issues is surely a step toward redressing the balance.

Of course, critics suggest that the televangelists have merely contributed to the further privatization of the public sphere. What kind of society is it, they ask, when we become so obsessed with Gary Hart's sex life that we cannot consider his potential as a political candidate on the basis of the issues themselves? Or hasn't television in general done us a disservice by emphasizing the president's hernias more than the negotiations for an arms agreement?

Those criticisms, however, have more to do with personality politics than with the publicizing of private concerns. They glamorize politics and give us unrealistic role models in the same way that Hollywood does. But if religion does have an intensely private dimension—if it is concerned with repentance and forgiveness, with redemption and sorrow, with morality and devotion—then it may not be an altogether negative development to see some of these private issues modeled and made the subject of public discussion.

To summarize, I have argued that religious television has both a private and a public dimension. In evaluating its cultural impact, we must consider the *quality* of its impact in both these realms. We want some aspects of religious devotion to be intensely private. We expect individuals to use their religious imaginations and to personalize their faith by tailoring it to their own experiences. Sitting alone in one's living room before the television, one may be able to do that. But we must also consider the consequences of religious television promoting a purely passive, unspontaneous, and unimaginative style of faith.

We may also discover that religious television gives people something to talk about with their friends and makes them feel part of some broader religious or political movement. In that sense, religious television viewing cannot be considered a strictly private affair. Nevertheless, it is the quality of this interaction with which we must concern ourselves. We must consider the kind of faith that results from listening to a single authoritative voice, as opposed to engaging in open dialogue with fellow believers who may represent a wide variety of views and experiences.

It is, then, important to consider the pluses and minuses associated with bringing public personalities, such as Jerry Falwell, into our living rooms, and with taking private issues, such as sexuality or forgiveness, into the public realm. Of course, some way to bridge the two realms is vital to the functioning of any society. We must, however, be careful about the ways in which the two are interrelated. Too much privatization of the public realm contributes to the narcissism that already plays a prominent role in our culture. Too much infusing of the public into our private lives constitutes a potential violation of our personal rights and our sense of personal integrity. Indeed, it is perhaps this sense of violation—the intrusion of such public faces as Jerry Falwell and Pat Robertson into our private lives—that has been behind much of the annoyance that the public has begun to register toward the televangelists.[5]

The following lines, penned by W. H. Auden, seem to provide a fitting commentary on the delicate balance between the public and the private—the balance that religious television influences in so many ways:

5. As one indication of the negative sentiment, a 1987 Harris poll showed that 77 percent of the American public agreed with the statement, "The TV evangelical movement has been harmful to the conservative cause, has made a mockery of what religion should be, and has taken advantage of millions of followers by urging them to give their money"; reported in *Index to International Public Opinion, 1986-1987* (Westport, CT: Greenwood Press, 1988), p. 477.

Private faces in public places
Are wiser and nicer
Than public faces in private places.[6]

THE EFFECTS OF SOCIAL RESTRUCTURING

Finally, how have the broader changes which have taken place in American society since World War II—the growth of the state, educational expansion, and the culture of technology—shaped the character of religious television? Can the social aspects of religious television be understood within the same matrix of developments that have restructured American religion more generally?

The direct effect of the state on religious television can be seen in the FCC and IRS regulations to which television programming is subject. Because television is subject to federal regulations and because religious programs raise millions of dollars from nationwide audiences, the televangelists stand in a much more vulnerable position relative to the state than most clergy ever have. Local churches may feel the effects of zoning laws and local clergy may be active in community politics, but seldom are they as likely as the televangelists to run up against direct federal restrictions.

The direct effects of technology on religious television can also be seen not only in its usage of satellite hookups, cable channels, WATS lines, and computerized direct-mailing services, but also in the content of its message. As Marshall McLuhan taught us to recognize, television is a "cool medium" in which intimate conversation, relaxed discussion, and humor play a more effective role than fiery rhetoric and a loud voice. Fulton Sheen became the master of this new style in the 1950s.

One would wonder how much the televangelists have learned about this style when considering the traditional tent-meeting approach of a Jimmy Swaggart or Rex Humbard. Nevertheless, it is evident from even a casual viewing of religious television that a number of the leading televangelists—Pat Robertson and Jim Bakker, for example—have succeeded by abandoning the hot rhetoric of a Billy Sunday for the cool demeanor of a Johnny Carson. Even Jerry Falwell, still the angry preacher arousing the masses from damnation,

6. Quoted in Anthony Arblaster, *The Rise and Decline of Western Liberalism* (Oxford: Basil Blackwell, 1984), p. 45.

has learned the value of an intimate heart-to-heart chat taped in his private office.

The effect of such social factors on the religious broadcasters, however, is less worthy of attention than the effect of these factors on the religious television audience. Viewers of religious television are not located simply at random with respect to the broader society. They exhibit distinctive social attributes which reveal the changes that have been taking place in American religion.

It is well to recognize in the first instance that religious television viewers are extremely diverse both socially and religiously. For example, despite the fact that many of the leading broadcasts come from southern states, almost two out of every three viewers live in other parts of the country. Many viewers are white Protestants, but about one in five is black and an equal number are Roman Catholics. Many are evangelicals, according to the way Gallup surveys define this concept, but by the same standards 63 percent do not qualify as evangelicals and as many as 33 percent are associated with mainline Protestant denominations, such as Methodists, Lutherans, Presbyterians, or Episcopalians. Nevertheless, in comparison with the social characteristics of nonviewers, there are some distinct differences.

As might be expected, viewers are much more likely than nonviewers to share evangelical or conservative religious convictions. In a national survey, for example, the belief that "the Bible is the actual word of God and is to be taken literally, word for word," was held by 58 percent of the viewers, compared with only 28 percent of the nonviewers. Similarly, more than half of the viewers (55 percent), compared with only a quarter (24 percent) of the nonviewers, described themselves as having been "born again." Since the largest religious broadcasting organizations emphasize evangelical themes, this characteristic of the religious television audience should come as no surprise.

Predictably, religious television viewers were also distinguished from nonviewers by virtue of being heavy viewers of conventional television. Within each level of religiosity, respondents who watched four or more hours of conventional television a day were at least five percentage points more likely to have watched a religious program in the past thirty days than were persons who watched conventional television less than two hours a day. The former were also more likely to have watched religious programs at least two hours during the past week than were the latter.

These characteristics are interesting less in themselves than for what they suggest about the social strata from which religious viewers are likely to be recruited. Most studies find that persons who watch conventional television in high amounts tend to be older than average and less well educated. Persons who hold evangelical beliefs tend to be drawn from the same social strata. The religious television audience thus reflects the combination of both these effects.

In the national survey, 48 percent of the viewers were age 50 or older, compared with only 31 percent of the nonviewers. Only 23 percent of the viewers had ever been to college, compared with 34 percent of the nonviewers. Despite the fact that age is associated with lower probabilities of having been to college, both factors were significantly related to religious viewing. For example, 52 percent of the persons in the study who were age 50 or over and who had no more than a grade school education had watched religious television in the past month, compared with only 25 percent of those in the same age group with college degrees. In the age bracket comprising 30- to 49-year-olds, 50 percent of the grade school educated had watched, compared with 22 percent of the college graduates. In the 18-to-30-year-old category, where too few had only grade school educations to make valid comparisons possible, 21 percent of the high school graduates had watched compared with only 13 percent of the college graduates.

In terms of broader social changes, then, in which education becomes an increasingly important measure of standing and social resources, religious television viewers tend relatively to be recruited from among the dispossessed. Very few are young people with college educations; most are older people with lower levels of education.

The study also demonstrated an important connection between religious viewing and dissatisfaction with the moral climate of the nation. For example, among nonviewers only 31 percent said they were very dissatisfied with "the way moral standards have been changing in America," but among viewers this proportion rose to 50 percent—and most of the remainder said they were somewhat dissatisfied.

If we piece the various findings together, it seems clear that religious television has come to occupy a distinct niche in American society that in turn reflects some of the broader changes that have been shaping social relations over the past several decades. Its audience is located among relatively less advantaged segments of the population who also identify with conservative religious ideas and who feel unhappy with the moral direction in which they believe the culture is heading. One might note that all of these characteristics reinforce one another, but each contributes somewhat independently to the likelihood of being a religious viewer as well. One should also note that the same characteristics distinguish those who watch religious programs frequently from those who watch less frequently, and those who donate money to these programs from those who do not.

THE REINFORCEMENT OF RELIGIOUS CLEAVAGE

The growth of religious television has led critics to worry vocally about its potentially negative effects on the local church. Those fears for the most part have proved to be unwarranted. But the critics have failed to foresee a deeper ramification of televangelism. It was, perhaps inevitably, destined to attract the widest audiences among those who already spent unusual amounts of time watching television and whose devout commitment to traditional religion was sufficient to motivate their time, energy, and financial contributions toward the televangelists. This was the natural audience—the niche of convenience—to which religious television became tailored. And there were plenty of funds, plenty of preachers, and plenty of viewers to make it work.

But the natural audience for religious television was also a socially dispossessed segment of the society. Despite its more visible aspirants among the national elite, it was relatively concentrated among the elderly and the less educated. If for no other reason than the fact that television and evangelical religion intersected to form this audience, it was largely devoid of representation among the better-educated sector of the secular elite. Thus, an additional element found its way increasingly into the message of the televangelists.

That element was the message of moral reconstruction. The dispossessed provided a sufficiently large pool of religious viewers that their sense of moral erosion came to be expressed in the appeals of religious programming. Not surprisingly, the programs appealed to those who felt the moral order was on the skids. At the same time, this selective process drove an ever larger wedge between religious television and those with other religious convictions, and between the morally concerned Religious Right and those among the secular elite.

Religious television was clearly an important resource for the disadvantaged evangelical. It not only provided personal religious gratifications in a world that seemed otherwise awry, but it also created a sense that one was participating in something broader—that perhaps the moral order could be saved. Religious television did not replace the local church. It merely created an umbrella under which the remnant of God's people could come together, if only symbolically, for renewal and strength.

The shelter provided by that umbrella was no less genuine to those who experienced it because it was transmitted via communication satellite than if it had been created in a local revival meeting. It was, however, a shelter that failed to convey meaning for most who looked across the cultural chasm from their position in the liberal churches, the universities, and high-tech institutions of the secular society. For them, religious television was not so much a shelter as a stumbling block. It was simply yet another cultural barrier which divided American religion.

Seven   Science and the Sacred

FOR MORE THAN A CENTURY, the claims of science have been hotly disputed in American religion. Evangelicals and fundamentalists have often reacted to new discoveries and theories with misgiving, while religious liberals have embraced them enthusiastically. In recent years, the two wings of American Christianity have again found themselves at odds with one another over such issues as creation and evolution, genetic testing, and definitions of the beginning of life.

Most discussions of the relations between religion and science have been heavily influenced by assumptions about the increasingly secular character of American culture. In particular, it is often posited that the rapid expansion of modern science and the dissemination of a scientific attitude among the general public will result in an erosion of conventional religious commitments.

It is also common to hear arguments that this erosion is due to such self-evident conflicts between science and religion as the proverbial "warfare" between reason and faith, between the results of modern astronomy and the medieval religious conception of a three-tiered universe, between evolutionary theory and biblical creationist views, between the causal determinism of science and the espousal of individual free will (and, hence, responsibility) by religion, or more broadly, between the cognitive and positivistic approaches to knowledge of the sciences and the subjective or hermeneutic orientations found in most contemporary religious perspectives. According to these arguments, secularization comes about as a result of direct conflict between religion, which appears to consist largely of beliefs about the nature of reality, and science, which offers different interpretations of the same phenomena.

THE RELATION BETWEEN RELIGION AND SCIENCE

In efforts to see whether these arguments are valid, a wide variety of evidence has been examined over the past half-century. The conclusion drawn from this evidence is that it shows unqualified support for the religion/science conflict thesis.

The clearest support has come from studies of scientists and academicians themselves. Unlike the general public, they are assumed to have actually thought seriously enough about science, and to have grasped its implications well enough, to have had it influence their religious views. One of the first quantitative studies of religious views ever conducted was psychologist James Leuba's examination of the religious beliefs of scientists listed in the 1913-1914 edition of *American Men of Science*.[1] This study showed that scientists tended less than other professionals to believe in God or in immortality, and that faculty members were less likely to hold these beliefs than were nonacademicians.

More recent studies have generally confirmed these results. A study of data from a national survey of graduate students found them to be nonreligious in far greater proportion than the general public and demonstrated negative relationships between religious involvement and a variety of scholarly orientations, including attendance at high-quality graduate and undergraduate schools, cosmopolitanism, identifying oneself as an intellectual, and valuing self-expression.[2] Another analysis of these data confirmed the relation between low religiosity and intellectualism and also showed that the less religious students feel alienated in general from nonacademic settings.[3]

1. James Leuba, *The Belief in God and Immortality* (Boston: Sherman French & Company, 1916); idem, "Religious Beliefs of American Scientists," *Harper's Magazine* 169 (August 1934): 291-300.

2. See Rodney Stark, "On the Incompatibility of Religion and Science," *Journal for the Scientific Study of Religion* 3 (1963): 3-20.

3. See Jan Hajda, "Alienation and Integration of Student Intellectuals," *American Sociological Review* 26 (1961): 758-77.

Another graduate-student survey found a positive correlation between religious apostasy and a preference for academic careers.[4] An analysis of national data on faculty members collected by the Carnegie Commission in the late 1960s revealed a negative relation between religiosity and university quality, and found that the less religious were more likely to identify themselves as intellectuals, preferred research over other academic activities, and published more.[5] Another analysis of these data showed the latter findings to hold true when differences in specialties were taken into account.[6] Finally, a survey of faculty members in a midwestern city, designed especially to examine religious commitment, found negative relations between the ideological, ritual, and experiential dimensions of religious commitment and various measures of scholarly orientation, including identification with one's field and valuing research, in both nonsectarian and sectarian schools.[7]

Some additional evidence which appears to support these earlier studies was provided by the *Connecticut Mutual Life Report on American Values in the '80s*, a national study conducted in 1980, which included interviews with randomly selected "leaders" in a variety of institutional areas, among which was "science."[8] In comparison with the general public, scientists were far less likely to indicate religious involvement. Only 31 percent said they frequently felt that God loves them, compared with 73 percent of the general public. Only 8 percent of the scientists had frequently had a religious experience, compared with 25 percent of the public. Sixty-four percent of the scientists had ever read the Bible, compared with 75 percent of the public. Only 28 percent of the scientists said they attended church frequently, compared with 44 percent of the public. Twenty-seven percent said they prayed frequently, compared with 57 percent of the public. Eighteen percent said they had made a personal commitment to Christ, com-

4. See Joseph Zelan, "Religious Apostasy, Higher Education, and Occupational Choice," *Sociology of Education* 41 (1968): 370-79; see also Charles A. Salter and Lewis M. Routledge, "Intelligence and Belief in the Supernatural," *Psychological Reports* 34 (1974): 299-302; and Douglas F. Campbell and Dennis W. Magill, "Religious Involvement and Intellectuality Among University Students," *Sociological Analysis* 29 (1968): 79-93.

5. See Stephen Steinberg, *The Academic Melting Pot: Catholics and Jews in American Higher Education* (New York: McGraw-Hill, 1974).

6. See Michael A. Faia, "The Myth of the Liberal Professor," *Sociology of Education* 47 (1974): 171-202; see also idem, "Secularization and Scholarship Among American Professors," *Sociological Analysis* 37 (1976): 63-74.

7. See Edward C. Lehman, Jr., "The Scholarly Perspective and Religious Commitment," *Sociological Analysis* 33 (1972): 199-213.

8. Research and Forecasts, Inc., New York, 1981.

pared with 47 percent of the public. And 50 percent thought they were religious persons, compared with 74 percent of the public.

Some of these differences may have been due to the fact that educational levels of leaders are generally higher than those of the public. Nevertheless, even among the leaders sampled, scientists scored at the very bottom of the list on virtually every question about religion.

Although these kinds of studies represent the most straightforward tests of the religion/science conflict thesis (in that they focus on scientists and academicians themselves), a variety of other evidence also appears to lend indirect support to the thesis. For instance, virtually all surveys and polls, whether of the general public, college students, church members, or clergy, show inverse relations between exposure to higher education and adherence to core religious tenets, such as the existence of God, the divinity of Christ, the divine inspiration of the Bible, life after death, religious conversion, and the necessity of faith in Christ for salvation. None of these studies has actually proven that exposure to science is the reason why the better educated turn out to have lower measures of religious commitment. But this has generally been assumed to be a factor.

Other research has indicated the differences in life-styles and attitudes associated with scientific or social scientific meaning systems as opposed to theistic meaning systems. In particular, the former appear to be considerably more willing, at least in the present cultural context, to experiment with social reform and with alternative life-styles or leisure activities in their personal lives than the latter.[9]

Cross-national studies have shown, perhaps obviously, that growth in scientific knowledge has led religion to represent a declining share of scholarly output in many modern and modernizing countries.[10]

As another indication of the potential for perceived trade-offs between science and religion, 89 percent of a national sample identified "scientific research" as making a major contribution to America's greatness; by comparison, only 57 percent listed "deep religious beliefs" in this role.[11] Another survey showed that 46 percent of the public thought

9. See Robert Wuthnow, *The Consciousness Reformation* (Berkeley and Los Angeles: University of California Press, 1976); see also Angela A. Aidala, "Worldviews, Ideologies and Social Experimentation: Clarification and Replication of 'The Consciousness Reformation,'" *Journal for the Scientific Study of Religion* 24 (1984): 111-23.

10. See Robert Wuthnow, "A Longitudinal, Cross-National Indicator of Cultural Religious Commitment," *Journal for the Scientific Study of Religion* 16 (1977): 87-99.

11. National Science Foundation, *Science Indicators, 1980* (Washington, D.C.: U.S. Government Printing Office, 1981), p. 337.

"technological know-how" contributes most to the influence of the United States in the world, whereas only 15 percent thought the same about "our religious heritage."[12] Similar studies over the past decade have shown rising levels of faith in science at the same time that confidence in religion's ability to solve major problems has declined.[13] Numerous historical studies have focused on the declining significance of religion in areas ranging from schoolbooks and popular fiction to medicine and law as scientific theories and evidence have become accepted as standard criteria of truth or professional practice in place of religious worldviews.[14]

SOME ANOMALIES

Despite the seemingly overwhelming nature of the evidence supporting the idea of conflict between religion and science, some peculiar aspects of the research results do not seem to fit very well into the conventional view of this relationship.

For one thing, it appears historically that there was a positive relation between religion, particularly Puritanism, in the seventeenth and eighteenth centuries and the rise of science itself, or so sociologist Robert Merton argued in a famous thesis.[15] In the United States, many prominent scientists in the past were devout Christians, and the institutions in which they worked were often sponsored by leading religious denominations.

Contemporarily, there is the fact that the more scientific disciplines, such as physics and chemistry, usually have higher levels of religiosity among their practitioners than do the less scientific specialties, such as the social sciences or the humanities. For instance, the Carnegie data on faculty members showed that 49 percent of faculty

12. See Jon D. Miller, Kenneth Prewitt, and Robert Pearson, *The Attitudes of the U.S. Public Toward Science and Technology* (Chicago: National Opinion Research Center, University of Chicago, 1980), pp. 251-53.

13. See National Science Foundation, *Science Indicators, 1980*, p. 335; George H. Gallup, Jr., *Religion in America, 1982* (Princeton: Princeton Religion Research Center, 1982).

14. See Ruth Miller Elson, *Guardians of Tradition: American Schoolbooks of the Nineteenth Century* (Lincoln: University of Nebraska Press, 1964); Louis Schneider and Sanford M. Dornbusch, *Popular Religion* (Chicago: University of Chicago Press, 1958); and Earl R. Babbie, *Science and Morality in Medicine: A Survey of Medical Educators* (Berkeley and Los Angeles: University of California Press, 1970).

15. Robert K. Merton, *Science, Technology and Society in Seventeenth-Century England* (New York: Harper & Row, 1970).

in the social sciences were indifferent or opposed to religion, compared with 46 percent in the humanities, 41 percent in the biological sciences, and only 37 percent in the physical sciences.[16] Another study of faculty members showed similar patterns: 41 percent of the social scientists did not believe in God, compared with 36 percent of those in the humanities and 20 percent in the natural sciences; similarly, 48 percent, 45 percent, and 34 percent, respectively, said they never attended church.[17] Several studies of graduate students and a host of undergraduate surveys also reveal these patterns.[18] In other words, the ordering of the disciplines is wrong: if science really conflicted with religious commitment, we would expect the natural sciences to have the least commitment and the humanities or social sciences to have the most; but the opposite is the case.

Many of the studies done among students and aspiring scientists or academicians also indicate that it is the irreligious who enter into academic careers in the first place, not that the process of being socialized into the academic life causes them to become less and less religious as time goes on. For example, data from students at the University of California, Berkeley, suggests that religious nonconventionality—indeed, nonconventionality in general—leads subsequently to higher academic performance and identification with the intellectual role, even when earlier measures of academic standing were taken into account. But the data show no tendency for high academic performance or intellectualism to result in subsequent shifts toward religious nonconventionality. In short, the conflict between religion and academic careers does not seem to occur as part of the socialization process into those careers, but *prior to it*.[19]

Again, there are some striking differences by discipline. In the Berkeley data, those majoring in the social sciences were most likely to have been raised in nonreligious families, humanities students were most likely to have defected from the religion in which they were brought up, and natural science students were more likely to have retained their religious faith.

16. See Steinberg, *Academic Melting Pot*.

17. See Fred Thalheimer, "Religiosity and Secularization in the Academic Professions," *Sociology of Education* 46 (1973): 183-202.

18. For example, see Kenneth A. Feldman and Theodore M. Newcomb, *The Impact of College on Students* (San Francisco: Jossey-Bass, 1970).

19. Results from an unpublished analysis of panel data collected among freshmen and senior males in 1971 and 1973; see Robert Wuthnow, *Experimentation in American Religion* (Berkeley and Los Angeles: University of California Press, 1978).

Perhaps more to the point, a study that sought to determine why some students choose to embark on careers as college professors found that religiosity was not a factor affecting the choices of students in the natural sciences, but it was an important factor in the choices of social sciences and humanities students.[20] The point is that people in the natural sciences not only have higher levels of religiosity later in life than do their counterparts in the social sciences and the humanities but are also less deterred by religiosity from embarking on these careers in the first place.

Also problematic is the fact that longitudinal evidence in the United States over the past several decades reveals very little tendency for the rapid growth in science to have been accompanied by an equally dramatic decline in religious commitment. The growth in science and, more generally, in higher education and in other professions since World War II has been nothing short of spectacular: quantitative indices show that expenditures for Research and Development increased from $6 billion in 1955 to $61 billion in 1980, and adjusting for inflation, this was still a rise of more than 300 percent.[21] Over the same period, the number of college or advanced degrees conferred annually rose from about 350,000 to about 1,300,000; expenditures on higher education grew from about $2 billion to more than $50 billion annually; the proportion of young people enrolled in higher education tripled; and the average level of educational attainment rose by almost three full years. As early as the mid-1960s, the United States had more than half a million research scientists in the labor force, the highest proportion of any country in the world; it produced almost 40 percent of all scientific and technical articles in the world; and almost two-thirds of its exports were produced by industries that relied heavily on science and technology.[22] But over the same period, quantitative indices of institutional religion held remarkably steady; church membership hovered at about 60 percent; clergy and religious workers made up about the same proportion of the labor force that they had for the past fifty years; the number of nonprofit religious organizations held its own as a proportion of all

20. See Ian D. Currie, Henry C. Finney, Travis Hirschi, and Hannan C. Selvin, "Images of the Professor and Interest in the Academic Profession," *Sociology of Education* 39 (1966): 301-23.

21. See National Science Foundation, *Science Indicators, 1980* (Washington, D.C.: U.S. Government Printing Office, 1980).

22. See *U.S. Statistical Abstract, 1981* (Washington, D.C.: U.S. Bureau of the Census, 1981); National Science Foundation, *Science Indicators, 1978* (Washington, D.C.: U.S. Government Printing Office, 1978).

such organizations; and, although church attendance dropped slightly, most of this decline seemed to be a function of changes in morality and life-styles rather than exposure to science.

Finally, cross-sectional studies of the public and of religious groups have shown that individuals have a remarkable propensity actually to *mix* religious and scientific worldviews. For instance, Gallup polls asking about creation and evolution show that the largest segment of the public adheres to some combination of these views (only a small fraction believes exclusively in evolution). Other studies in both the United States and Canada show that people frequently mix theistic and scientific or positivistic understandings.[23] Case studies have also shown that religious groups and movements of all theological varieties have a pronounced tendency to rely heavily on scientific evidence and testimony to *support* their religious claims.[24]

SOME AD HOC REVISIONS OF THE ARGUMENT

These anomalies have not gone unnoticed in the literature on religion and science. Their implication, at least on the surface, seems devastating to the notion that religion and science are locked in some inevitable struggle to the death. To defend this traditional notion, a number of counterarguments and ad hoc revisions of the basic thesis have been put forth.

Robert Merton's argument relating Puritanism and the development of science has been roundly attacked on the basis of more elaborate historical evidence and cross-national comparisons. Even defenders of the argument point out that a relationship between Puritanism and science that was originally positive does not rule out the possibility of conflict arising between the two once science became fully institutionalized.[25]

23. See Gallup, *Religion in America, 1982;* Wuthnow, *The Consciousness Reformation;* and Reginald W. Bibby, "Religion and Modernity: The Canadian Case," *Journal for the Scientific Study of Religion* 18 (1979): 1-17.

24. See Eileen Barker, "Thus Spake the Scientist: A Comparative Account of the New Priesthood and Its Organisational Bases," *Annual Review of the Social Sciences of Religion* 3 (1979): 79-103.

25. Critical studies of this relationship include Richard L. Greaves, "Puritanism and Science: The Anatomy of a Controversy," *Journal of the History of Ideas* 33 (1969): 345-68; A. Rupert Hall, "Merton Revisited: Science and Society in the 17th Century," *History of Science* 11 (1963): 1-16; Lotte Mulligan, "Civil War Politics, Religion and the Royal Society," *Past and Present* 59 (1973): 92-116; and Robert Wuthnow, "The World-Economy

On the issue of the social sciences and humanities showing more religious apostasy than the natural sciences, an intriguing argument has been advanced which suggests that the conflict is more pronounced in the former than in the latter precisely because the latter enjoys more "scholarly distance" from religion. In other words, social scientists and humanists study religion itself and therefore run into a conflict of paradigms, whereas the natural sciences usually do not study religion.[26] The same argument could apparently be applied to the evidence on early selection patterns among aspiring academicians.

The evidence on long trends in religion and science is easiest to refute by pointing to *attitudinal* data on religion which suggest that religiosity has in fact declined sharply over the past thirty years. For instance, Gallup polls conducted since the early 1950s show significant declines in the percentages of people who believe religion can answer their problems, who say religion is important in their personal lives, who pray, and who think religion's influence in society is increasing.

From a different perspective, the evidence of people mixing religion and science has been interpreted as evidence of a secularizing tendency itself; namely, that science has begun to penetrate previously sacred realms and, in the future, will likely dominate these realms to an even greater extent. At present, therefore, the idea that science is eroding religion as part of a broader and inevitable secularization process is by no means without defenders. And a large share of these defenders work primarily in the sociology of religion.

To be sure, some in sociology and in religious studies have sought to circumvent the secularization perspective by reconceptualizing religion and its functions in such a way that it avoids any appearance of inevitable conflict with science. If religion consists of a special kind of symbolism whose purpose is to evoke the wholeness of life, as Robert Bellah has argued, or if it mediates between worldviews and our everyday ethos, in Clifford Geertz's terms, or is, more importantly, faith rather than belief, as Wilfred Cantwell Smith has suggested, then clearly its conflict with science should be minimal.[27]

---

and the Institutionalization of Science in Seventeenth-Century Europe," in *Studies of the Modern World-System,* ed. Albert Bergesen (New York: Academic Press, 1980), pp. 25-55.

26. See Edward C. Lehman and Donald W. Shriver, Jr., "Academic Discipline as Predictive of Faculty Religiosity," *Social Forces* 47 (1968): 171-82.

27. Robert N. Bellah, *Beyond Belief* (New York: Harper & Row, 1970); Clifford Geertz, *The Interpretation of Cultures* (New York: Harper & Row, 1973); Wilfred Cantwell Smith, *Faith and Belief* (Princeton: Princeton University Press, 1979).

The key phrase, however, is "should be." What these arguments have done is to posit ways of reconciling religion and science
at a highly intellectual level or in the far distant future, rather than address the conflicts that may in fact presently exist. It has been, ironically, from the sociology of science, rather than from the sociology of
religion, that the most telling challenges to the traditional secularization view have taken place.

In essence, many of the workers in sociology of science have
recently begun to take seriously the idea that science is a socially constructed reality, just as other forms of knowledge and belief are. Accordingly, heavy emphasis has been placed on the ways in which scientific work and the products of that work reflect the social environment
in which they occur.

Approaches vary from the so-called strong programme, represented best in Scottish sociology of science, which argues that even
simple and seemingly irrefutable scientific facts, such as two plus two
equals four, are really reflections of social experience; to the new "an-
thropology of science," which examines the social processes involved
in the laboratory to elicit consensus and the structure of scientific discourse; to theories of scientific method which debunk textbook descrip-
tions of scientific procedure as being post hoc reconstructions and
which argue for an anarchistic approach to science.[28]

While none of these approaches has yet addressed the relation between religion and science directly, they have laid the groundwork for such a reexamination by relativizing the reality (the sacred-
ness) of science. Whereas the conventional view of this relation,
adopted from secularization theory, has tended to view science as an
unquestionable description of fact, against which religious belief has
inevitably been put to rout, the more recent view of science suggests
it to be a precarious reality in need of constant social reconstruction
and reaffirmation. From this perspective, the relation between science
and religion may be reconceptualized as a kind of reality-maintaining
process as far as science itself is concerned.

28. Among the more important of these studies are Barry Barnes, *Scientific
Knowledge and Sociological Theory* (London: Routledge & Kegan Paul, 1974); David Bloor,
"Two Paradigms for Scientific Knowledge?" *Science Studies* 1 (1971): 101-15; Paul
Feyerabend, *Against Method* (London: Verso, 1970); Bruno Latour and Steve Woolgar,
Laboratory Life: The Social Construction of Scientific Facts (Princeton: Princeton University
Press, 1987); and Michael Mulkay, *The Word and the World* (Oxford: Oxford University
Press, 1986).

SCIENCE AS A CONSTRUCTED REALITY

The precariousness of science can be demonstrated from a source more
familiar to many students of religion than the recent work of construc-
tivists in science—namely, Alfred Schutz's famous essay on multiple
realities.[29] In this essay, which Peter Berger, Thomas Luckmann, and
others have drawn on as a basis for their interpretations of religion,
Schutz draws a sharp contrast between "scientific theorizing"—an instance of what he called a "finite province of meaning"—and the
paramount reality of everyday life.

Specifically, according to Schutz, scientific theorizing is non-
pragmatic, universalistic, governed by norms of personal detachment,
oriented toward the past and future of the problem at hand, revocable
in the sense that hypotheses are subject to constant revision, and dominated by an attitude of critical skepticism. By comparison, everyday
reality is pragmatic, particularistically oriented to the here and now of
the individual, governed by norms of self-interested involvement
("wide-awakeness"), oriented toward standard linear time, irrevocable,
and dominated by a "willing suspension of doubt." In short, there is
a fundamental opposition between the norms of science and the norms
governing conduct in everyday life.

Moreover, the practitioner of science is constrained to live in
both worlds, causing the sense of reality that accompanies one to fade
from view when living in the other, and vice versa. If the scientist is
to maintain the reality of science against the alternative and more
prevailing reality of everyday life, therefore, he or she must engage in
certain reality-maintaining activities. Indeed, the very quality of the
scientist's work is likely to depend on this reality-maintaining process.

One method by which science, like any reality, is maintained
is communication—the face-to-face interaction which Peter Berger has
labeled a "plausibility structure."[30] Not only do scientists frequently
communicate with other scientists to exchange ideas; but also their interaction reinforces, or helps them to maintain, the plausibility—the reality—of the scientific world. Studies show that this activity is a powerful predictor of both research productivity and scientific innovativeness.

A second mechanism of reality maintenance is the codification of a concise theoretical paradigm which specifies important re-

---

29. Alfred Schutz, "On Multiple Realities," in *Collected Papers,* vol. 1 (The
Hague: Nijhoff, 1962), pp. 209-59.
30. Peter L. Berger, *The Sacred Canopy* (Garden City, NY: Doubleday, 1967).

search problems, promotes communication, and clarifies standards of evaluation and reward. As Robert Merton and Harriet Zuckerman have observed, scientific disciplines vary widely in the degree to which codification has been achieved.[31] In disciplines such as the social sciences and the humanities, codification is low relative to the physical and biological sciences, resulting in wide variations among these disciplines, variations ranging from lower rates of communication in the social sciences and humanities, to greater variability in citations to the literature, to higher rejection rates in leading journals as a result of greater ambiguity concerning relevant problems and procedures. Thus, in the less codified disciplines some other mechanism of reality maintenance must be brought into play.

The argument I wish to suggest here is that scientists, especially those in the less codified disciplines, rely frequently on values, attitudes, and life-styles to maintain the reality of science by setting up *external boundaries* between themselves and the general public or those who represent the realm of everyday reality. In other words, scientists who lack clearly codified paradigms and strong communication networks turn to symbolic modes of differentiating themselves from everyday reality in order to maintain the plausibility of their scientific orientations—orientations that are inevitably precarious in relation to the paramount reality of everyday life. These "boundary-posturing mechanisms," to give them a name, create a diffuse social space in which the scientist can function and with which the scientist can identify as a person. To the extent that the scientist can maintain these boundaries, he or she is likely to be more productive, just like the scientist who relies on professional communication as a reality-maintaining device. Moreover, this boundary-posturing activity is likely to be especially important during the early process of socialization and entry into the scientific role.

IRRELIGIOSITY AS SCIENTIFIC BOUNDARY POSTURING

With this argument in hand, some of the anomalies observed earlier in the religion/science literature—anomalies that make little sense in terms of the standard secularization argument—can be interpreted

31. Robert K. Merton and Harriet Zuckerman, "Age, Aging, and Age Structure in Science," in *The Sociology of Science*, ed. Robert K. Merton (Chicago: University of Chicago Press, 1973), pp. 497-560.

more readily. Studies of the values and life-styles of scientists have shown them to differ consistently from nonscientists (and to vary in predictable ways from discipline to discipline) on a variety of characteristics, including political orientations, feelings of alienation, nonconventionality, and irreligiosity. Specifically, scientists usually turn out to be more politically liberal than the general public, express stronger feelings of personal alienation, and adopt nonconventional life-styles, in addition to their irreligiosity. Those in the social sciences and humanities are more likely to deviate from the general public on all these characteristics than are those in the natural sciences and applied disciplines. In the context of a more complete discussion of such patterns, it could probably be shown that all of these characteristics function as boundary-posturing mechanisms. In the present context, only the evidence on irreligiosity requires consideration.

It was observed earlier that academic scientists and graduate students in general are more likely to identify themselves as intellectuals, and more likely to value research and produce more scholarly work when they are irreligious than when they are religious. These findings can be interpreted to suggest that irreligiosity helps to maintain the plausibility of the scientific province by differentiating scientists (in their own minds at least) from the larger public who represent everyday reality and generally maintain stronger religious identifications. By helping to maintain the plausibility of the scientific role for the scientist, irreligiosity contributes to his or her role performance as a scientist, as indicated by higher productivity and greater attachment to the values of science.

The studies showing early irreligiosity leading to subsequent high levels of academic performance and to a likelihood of selecting academic careers point to the importance of this boundary-posturing mechanism during the selection and socialization process leading to scientific roles. Indeed, selection and early socialization appear to mark the critical stages as far as the relation between irreligiosity and science is concerned, because cohort comparisons of older scientists fail to show any tendency for extended work in science to result in declining levels of religious commitment (as the religion/science conflict hypothesis would predict). In short, the more successfully scientists can extricate themselves from the realm of everyday reality, of which conventional religion is an important aspect (at least in the United States), the more likely they are to make the transition successfully into the scientific role.

A more interesting anomaly that can also be given an interpretation from this point of view is the variation in irreligiosity by discipline; that is, why the most irreligious persons should be found in the *least scientific* disciplines, rather than in the most scientific disciplines. The high levels of irreligiosity observed in the social sciences and the humanities can be understood in terms of the *low levels of paradigmatic codification* in these disciplines and, therefore, the greater tendency of these disciplines to rely on boundary-posturing mechanisms such as irreligiosity.

As noted above, these disciplinary differences have been interpreted as being the result of differences in scholarly distance from religion, but this interpretation proves insufficient in itself, because it implies that people in the social sciences and humanities actually study religion (giving them low scholarly distance in comparison with practitioners of the natural sciences). In fact, this is not the case for the vast majority of persons in the social sciences or the humanities (in sociology, for example, fewer than 10 percent list sociology of religion as a specialty).

Furthermore, the logical extension of the scholarly distance argument leads to some strikingly implausible predictions: for example, that theologians and professors of religious studies will be the *least religious of all*, that political scientists will be most alienated from politics, and that family sociologists will be most likely to reject the family. The present interpretation is broader in that it suggests that people in the social sciences and humanities reject religion not so much because of what they dislike about religion specifically (otherwise, why should they also differ on political and life-style issues?), but because of the ill-codified reality which they need to protect within their own discipline.

Additional support for this interpretation comes from the fact that there is, indeed, greater boundary-maintaining activity among *religious people* in the social sciences and humanities than in the natural sciences. In Thalheimer's study of faculty members cited earlier, those in the social sciences and the humanities who *believed in God* were far more likely to say they had to keep their religious convictions and their research separate than those in the natural sciences who believed in God.[32] The natural scientists tended to say they did not have to keep the two realms separate. In other words, work in the social sciences and humanities needed to be protected from religious convictions; work in the physical sciences did not.

32. Fred Thalheimer, "Religiosity and Secularization in the Academic Professions," *Sociology of Education* 46 (1973): 183-202.

We should note that studies like this one typically show that people in the applied sciences and the professions resemble the natural scientists in religious convictions and, indeed, often display higher levels of religiosity. This pattern again is consistent with the idea of irreligiosity as a boundary-posturing mechanism. The applied sciences generally operate from better-codified paradigms than the social sciences and the humanities, according to Merton and Zuckerman's research, and, unlike the more purely academic disciplines, have less need to separate their reality from the reality of everyday life. Schutz specifically draws his distinction between pure scientific work (which he calls "scientific theorizing") and everyday reality, rather than between the application of scientific knowledge and everyday life.

Another feature of the religion/science relation which appears consistent with the boundary-posturing interpretation is that the general public, not being actively involved in maintaining the scientific role, can be (as it has in fact been shown to be) more eclectic about combining religious and scientific views. As numerous studies in other areas have demonstrated, the average person displays a high capacity for mixing beliefs which social scientists have been prone to regard as inconsistent. This is not to deny the inverse relation shown in most studies between people with high levels of education and religiosity, but these relations probably reflect broader socialization experiences, cohort differences, and the subculture of academia, more than they do direct exposure to science.

The other phenomenon that can be interpreted within the boundary-posturing framework is the fact that scientists seem more likely to think of themselves as religious persons than they are actually to engage in any of the conventional practices or beliefs associated with religion. This fact, coupled with (largely anecdotal) evidence of scientists and academicians pursuing idiosyncratic, syncretistic, and mystical religions or quasi-religions, suggests that scientists may be able to maintain private, nonconventional religious orientations at the same time that their public boundary-posturing activity calls on them to disassociate from the conventional religious performances that are tainted by everyday reality. An important conjectural implication of this tendency is that the broader cultural influence of higher education is likely to reinforce a privatized, diverse, "liberal" religious orientation, rather than a purely secular mode of life. That this reinforcement has been happening in American culture has, of course, been suggested in the previous chapters.

CONCLUSION

The evidence on religion and science, one of the areas in which the processes of advancing secularity should be most evident, points largely to the survival of religion in the postsecular era. While the evidence clearly documents the irreligiosity of scientists themselves, it shows that this irreligiosity is far more pronounced among the least scientific disciplines—the social sciences and humanities—than it is among the natural sciences. Closer inspection of the scientific role itself suggests that scientists in the social and humanistic disciplines may adopt an irreligious stance chiefly as one of the boundary-posturing mechanisms they use to distance themselves from the general public and, thereby, to maintain the precarious reality of the theorizing they do.

If this interpretation is correct, the proverbial conflict between religion and science may be more a function of the precariousness of science than of the precariousness of religion. Rather than religion being constantly on the run, so to speak, in the face of ever advancing scientific knowledge, scientists have had to carve out a space in which to work by dissociating themselves from the powerful claims religion has been able to make throughout history, and which it still appears to command over the everyday life of American society.

Eight The Costs of Marginality

IF PRACTITIONERS OF THE ACADEMIC DISCIPLINES—especially the social sciences—have taken a liberal or negative stance toward orthodox religion, one way in which the more conservative wing of American religion has responded has been to operate its own colleges. There is, of course, a long tradition of religious involvement in American higher education. But evangelical and fundamentalist colleges have continued to be founded in recent decades. Many of them offer students and faculty alike a haven from the harsh winds of antireligious sentiment that seem to prevail in many of the nation's leading academic departments and research universities.

It is to the faculty of these Christian colleges that many have looked for leadership in the current debates about theology, biblical interpretation, church-state relations, and specific issues such as abortion and school prayer. The perspectives that can be found on these campuses are highly diverse. They range from arch-fundamentalist (but politically passive) views, to aggressive combinations of fundamentalist doctrine and New Right politics, to evangelical and neo-orthodox perspectives shaded with hues of political liberalism. Even among the students and faculty of the leading evangelical colleges, much ferment and accommodation with the secular culture has been in evidence.[1]

1. See, for example, the provocative study by James Davison Hunter, *Evangelicalism: The Coming Generation* (Chicago: University of Chicago Press, 1987).

In the context of the present struggle between religious liberals and religious conservatives, the role of the evangelical colleges is especially important. The faculty at these institutions have opportunities to train the coming generation of evangelical pastors and denominational leaders. They also have opportunities to influence the current policies of their denominations through the writing and speaking they do. Beyond the sheer opportunity to make a difference, they also occupy an auspicious position in between the current extremes of religious liberalism and conservatism. On the one hand, by virtue of their commitment to the evangelical tradition, they are likely to remain sympathetic to many of the historic doctrines of religious conservatism. On the other hand, by virtue of their own educational attainment, their exposure to the liberal arts tradition, and their interaction with other members of the "knowledge elite," they are likely to have some affinity for liberal views.

Again, the ways in which individual faculty members may put together the various strands of liberal and conservative socio-theological tradition vary widely. But they are, on the whole, in a position to mediate between the more extreme versions of both. This may be particularly true of those at evangelical colleges who teach and do research in the social sciences. If any segment of the evangelical community has the opportunity to gain understanding of the present religious conflicts and to contribute to their resolution, it should be—or at least it should include—the social science faculties of the nation's evangelical colleges.

Whether the practitioners of these disciplines have the resources to make any real impact on the present debates is the question I wish to address in this chapter. Is their position at Christian colleges viable? From this position, can they contribute effectively to the ongoing research and writing in their disciplines? Can they bring a genuinely Christian perspective to the attention of their colleagues in the secular universities? With the specific opportunities and limitations they have, what style of research and writing is likely to be most effective?

SOME PRELIMINARY CONSIDERATIONS

Thinking about evangelical Christianity in relation to the social sciences is in many ways to engage in the depths of an intellectual contradiction. The founders of modern social science—Marx, Weber,

Durkheim—all abandoned any personal commitment to Christianity (or Judaism) long before they embarked on the intellectual journeys that produced their contributions to the formation of the social sciences. And if there is more diversity in the social sciences today than a century ago, little evidence would suggest that these disciplines' linkage with Christianity is a problem likely to interest many of its active practitioners. As some of the studies I quoted in the previous chapter suggest, it is probably safe to say that the majority of social scientists regard Christianity as a rather quaint legacy from the oral tradition of a largely agrarian society that has been perpetuated by a combination of church bureaucrats and popular insecurity, one that is ultimately of little importance to the main intellectual and social currents of society.

For their part, self-professed Christians in the broader society have been exposed to the social sciences in increasing doses, especially in larger denominations that have borrowed from the social sciences in conducting membership studies or as allies in developing social ministries. Evangelicals have also been exposed to the wonders of the social sciences through such inventions as the Gallup Poll and the popularizations of a Vance Packard or an Alvin Toffler.

Yet it is not impossible to discover that the two kingdoms, as it were, remain separated by a vast ocean of ignorance and misunderstanding—as I did recently in meeting a college-educated member of an evangelical church who, upon learning that I was a sociologist, informed me that he had real trouble relating to that and asked me to explain what exactly a sociologist did!

In view of the intellectual distance that seems to separate at least some manifestations of evangelical Christianity and the social sciences, one response that has been common among adherents of the two has been to attempt a reconciliation between them. In this vein, numerous discussions have been presented concerning the theoretical modifications in the social sciences that would presumably make them more compatible with Christianity. For example, some have proposed that social science would be more consistent with Christianity if deterministic assumptions were abandoned in favor of a more voluntaristic perspective. Others have argued for a greater emphasis on social conflict and disintegration in an effort to reconcile the study of society with Christianity's image of a broken society dominated by sinfulness. Still others have argued that social science as presently conceived is fundamentally flawed by its humanistic orientation and have called on Christians to rethink it from a more biblical foundation.

Whether these proposals have any merit remains to be seen. I would prefer to begin at a somewhat different starting place. Relative to the philosophical and metatheoretical discussions that have dominated the literature on the social sciences' relation to Christianity, little has been offered in the way of a concrete strategy for research and writing. Yet the fact remains that a sizable number of social scientists who regard themselves as evangelicals are not only engaged in research but are also anxious to expend their efforts in a way that is expressive of their religious convictions. What advice can be given?

An answer that must be considered, to be sure, is that the work in which a Christian academician engages should be no different from the activities in which any academician engages. This answer is defensible on two grounds. First, it is consistent with the idea that truth is truth, whether it be discovered by Christians, Jews, Buddhists, pagans, or anyone else. Second, it is consistent with the idea that any discipline is dominated by a kind of common knowledge about what is known and what is knowable, and therefore progresses best by puzzle solving within that framework. Though perhaps comforting to those who wish to follow the dictates of what is popular in the broader discipline, this answer fails to conform with most of what we now know about the ways in which academic knowledge comes to be produced.

The perspective from which the following argument is derived conceives of the research process in any discipline as a product of various social and cultural forces. I shall try to indicate what some of these forces are at present and then suggest some of the distinctive ways in which evangelical scholars may be affected by them. These considerations will provide the basis from which to outline some research strategies for the future and to offer some comments that may serve to motivate research along these lines.

SOCIAL INFLUENCES AND CHRISTIAN SCHOLARSHIP

Over the past decade or two, the social sciences have been profoundly affected by a general shift in epistemological understandings within the human sciences. This shift has involved an across-the-board questioning of the assumptions of empirical positivism and an increasing acceptance of the assumptions of hermeneutics. On the one hand, in its quest for universal, lawlike properties of human behavior that can be known objectively on the basis of scientific induction, positivism has proven to be a false hope in principle and little more than a crude heuristic in practice. Social behavior has persistently defied efforts at systematization and has repeatedly been shown to result in knowledge that can only be understood by taking into account the biases and presuppositions of the observer. Of course, methods of investigation and logic from the natural sciences still command a prominent place in the social sciences. But statistical controls, experimental designs, and systematic comparisons of observations fall far short of approximating the same conditions under which the natural sciences operate.

On the other hand, the assumptions of hermeneutics suggest that human behavior is inevitably subject to interpretation, that it must be understood within a situational context, and that lawlike patterns are never likely to exhaust the meaning of human behavior. Thus, at the same time that we continue to see quantitative data and statistical methods being emphasized, we are also able to witness a renewed interest in ethnographic and historical research that pays greater attention to the limitations of scientific inquiry that have been suggested by the hermeneutic tradition.

For the issue under consideration, this development has important implications. It means that values and worldviews cannot be separated from the research enterprise. Indeed, it is on this epistemological basis that the very call for greater diversity of research styles and perspectives has been made. To say that there must be a feminist political science, or a Marxist economics, or a gay sociology, is to say that implicit values and beliefs do in fact color the way in which research is done.

Now, these claims are always made within limits, of course. One must still follow certain canons of evidence and presentation in doing feminist studies: collect data as rigorously and systematically as possible, use methods of analysis that are appropriate to the problem at hand, state one's biases as clearly as possible, and defend one's conclusions with compelling logical argumentation. Having made all these concessions to the positivist tradition, we are still for the most part willing to say that a feminist perspective is likely to yield unique and valuable insights.

Furthermore, it has become part of the liberal arts tradition to welcome diverse perspectives into the arena of scholarly debate. We expect as part of that invitation that the representatives of each perspective will responsibly engage in interpretation and not be content with mere observation and reporting of alleged facts.

As I will try to point out later, there are conditions within the scholarly community that militate against Christian values and beliefs being accorded the same kind of acceptance as has been the case for feminism, Marxism, and a variety of other "isms." We can observe in passing that some of this resistance reflects doubts about evangelicals' commitment to the rules of interpretation and debate on which the hermeneutic method itself is established. Nevertheless, it is at least consistent with the broader shift in epistemology that I have described to say that Christian values can be regarded as one legitimate perspective from which to do academic work.

Let me hasten to say that one can make this case whether one regards Christian values as absolute truth or simply as a prominent subculture within the historical development of the modern world. The point is: an interpretative perspective that explicitly reflects the distinctive orientations and interests of Christians can be advanced as a legitimate enterprise. Within the understandings implicit in the hermeneutic method, a Christian view becomes one of several acceptable interpretations of human behavior.

To be sure, that may seem little consolation to those who would like Christian scholarship to be seen as the only true interpretation of human behavior. Even this somewhat relativistic vantage point is, however, a distinctly better position from which to operate than was the case under empirical positivism. Under that system only two kinds of argument were open to the Christian student of human behavior. One was the clearly pretentious view that only Christians could know the truth and therefore all secular scholarship in the human sciences (and by extension of the same argument all secular physics, medicine, and engineering) was false. The other was that knowledge was knowledge as long as it conformed to the canons of positivistic science—meaning that Christians had no reason at all to try to integrate their beliefs with the actual substance of their research. The advancing acceptance of the hermeneutic method suggests that Christian values, like any other values, will inevitably influence one's research and, moreover, that the interpretation will be richer if these values are explicitly recognized.

A second tendency within the academic community bodes less well for the interaction between Christian values and social research. In keeping with the emphasis on research as a product of social factors that I mentioned at the outset, we must bear in mind that knowledge is not simply the product of a free market of diverse arguments and opinions ("may the most convincing argument win"); it is the result of an enterprise that depends heavily on institutional resources. It takes place within academic institutions, which are in turn supported by endowments and tuition payments; it uses funds from the federal government, private foundations, and other sources; it is done by personnel who spent long years in training at certain kinds of institutions; it depends on graduate and undergraduate students for cheap labor in the initial production of research and as an audience to whom one can disseminate the results of this research; and it is always subject to the vagaries of the publishing industry, journal editors, and review panels.

It is no secret that these kinds of resources are highly stratified. For example, it has been calculated that for any discipline with a total given number of members who produce one article in a given period, the number of people in that discipline who will produce N articles in the same period is proportional to one divided by N-squared. Thus, in a discipline such as sociology with no more than about 5,000 members with full-time jobs in academic institutions, the number of active researchers who produce, say, three articles a year will be about 550 and the number who produce four articles will be about 300, if we assume that all 5,000 produce at least one article every year.[2] Much of the reason for this concentration is that the resources necessary to do research—especially time—are limited to those in a small number of institutions.

These considerations do not bode well for the relation between evangelical Christianity and scholarly research because institutional resources are not concentrated very heavily among Christian scholars. For example, if one surveys the membership of an organization such as the Christian Sociological Society, one sees a disproportionate concentration in small Christian colleges and in public institutions that are largely outside the ranks of the leading research universities.

This is not to say, necessarily, as some fundamentalist activists have charged in recent years, that the major research universities are nothing more than dens of wicked secular humanism. It does suggest, however, that those who would wish to see a distinctively evangelical scholarly orientation advanced are at a tremendous competitive disadvantage. To pit even the strong intellectual aspirations of a Wheaton College or a Calvin College, or the massive fund-raising network of a Liberty University, against the multibillion dollar endowments of a Princeton or a Harvard reveals the vast extent of this deficit in resources.

2. This formula is known as Lotka's Law. For a discussion, see Derek de Solla Price, *Science Since Babylon* (New Haven: Yale University Press, 1975), pp. 174-75.

The other general feature of the scholarly world to which I want to draw attention is in some ways a corollary of the last: academic scholarship is heavily influenced not only by the formal distribution of institutional resources but also by the informal networks that accompany these resources. Break the 500 (or even 1,500) active publishers in sociology down into a dozen or more substantive specialties and the number in each becomes quite small. Then concentrate most of this number at fifteen or twenty major research universities, give them virtually unlimited budgets for long-distance telephone calls, link them together by a single computerized BITNET hookup, get them together several times a year at conferences, put them on the same committees, and give them graduate students to trade around, and you have a fairly accurate picture of why informal networks play such a powerful role in shaping the discipline.

Moreover, for the most part these networks function very effectively. They provide the informal knowledge needed to know moment by moment what kinds of research questions are of interest to the leading members of each specialty. They serve as a basis for organizing conferences, putting together edited volumes and special issues of journals, and getting advice from interested parties. They greatly minimize the work involved in screening applicants for graduate school or for assistant professor jobs. And they function to certify some kinds of work and to give coherence to the research being produced in any given period.

The result is that some issues and orientations get "selected for" while others are "selected against," to use a biological metaphor. This means, as Thomas Kuhn pointed out some years ago, that a subdiscipline usually is in fact governed by some kind of "paradigm"—a paradigm that legitimates certain styles of research, dictates the questions that are important to try to answer, and even posits what the expected answers are.[3] For anyone on the fringes of the dominant networks, it becomes difficult to know what the paradigm is or why it is important.[4]

The implication of all this for the relation between evangelical Christianity and academic scholarship in the human sciences is perhaps

3. Thomas Kuhn, *The Structure of Scientific Revolutions,* 2nd ed. (Chicago: University of Chicago Press, 1970).

4. It is perhaps for this reason that students of science have also observed greater intellectual diversity on the fringes of established disciplinary networks; for example, see Ludwik Fleck, *Genesis and Development of a Scientific Fact* (Chicago: University of Chicago Press, 1979).

obvious. Nevertheless, let me make the obvious more painfully obvious by turning briefly to a more explicit consideration of the institutional base from which evangelical social science operates at present.

THE PROSPECTS FOR EVANGELICAL STUDIES

I suspect that the main interest in trying to conduct studies of human behavior from a distinctly Christian perspective comes from those who would identify themselves as *evangelicals*. But even more generally, I suspect that the audience for such studies consists primarily of evangelicals. Members of liberal mainline Protestant churches, Catholics, and those who for whatever reason have adopted a more privatized form of Christianity may well share some of the same values as evangelicals and may allow these values to influence their scholarly interests, but they have for the most part abstained from making Christianity a public or visible issue in relation to such interests.

In contrast, evangelicals have taken a much more distinctive approach to their own religious convictions. To be sure, there is much variation among evangelicals as to how their convictions become manifest. But at least some of the following are likely to be present: a desire to communicate the biblical message of salvation and to convert others to Christianity, a strong belief in the Bible as a unique touchstone for determining matters of truth and practice, an active commitment to some branch of the institutional church, and a desire to integrate all of one's activities and thoughts as consistently as possible around one's religious convictions.

What this means is that the call for relating Christianity to scholarship reflects something other than a vague, diverse, least-common-denominator interpretation of the Christian faith; it reflects the distinctive subculture of American evangelical Christianity. And we know from studies of the evangelical community that it is indeed a distinctive subculture in many ways.

In comparison with the rest of the population, and certainly in comparison with the population of academic faculty in the social sciences, the evangelical subculture tends to be more conservative on most moral issues, disproportionately pro-life rather than pro-choice (although both views are represented), somewhat more conservative on gender issues such as ordination of women and views of the Equal Rights Amendment, more fearful of communism, more devoted to the principles of free enterprise in business, more suspicious of big government, and more supportive of strong national defenses.[5]

To go back to my earlier point about the hermeneutic perspective, these differences mean that evangelicals, as scholars, are likely to approach their subject matter from a perspective that is indeed distinct—not simply in terms of religious views but on a whole range of moral, social, economic, and political issues as well.

I do not wish to focus on any of these specific issues but to make the general point that evangelicals who attempt to integrate Christianity and scholarship will inevitably bring along their own subculture as well. Not only is their interpretation of Christianity one of many, but their views of society will be colored by their social backgrounds, peers, life-styles, and secular values as well.

It is for this reason, I believe, that many Christians and non-Christians outside the evangelical subculture feel that evangelicals' appropriation of the term "Christian" without necessary qualifications is pretentious. A more accurate designation might, in fact, be "evangelical scholarship" rather than "Christian scholarship."

Once one recognizes that any attempt to do scholarly work from an evangelical standpoint must reflect the entire evangelical subculture, one is likely to see the resultant product as having both its strong points and its pitfalls. One strong point is that evangelicals probably do have something distinctive to bring to the human sciences. I will come to some of those in a moment. The pitfall is that evangelicals may be no more likely to discover the pure, absolute truth in their research than, say, feminist sociologists or Marxist economists. Hopefully some approximations to the truth come closer than others. But healthy skepticism is clearly in order if anyone advances "the Christian truth" about sociology or anything else.

In keeping with the previous observations about the institutional locations of scholarly research, we must also say something about evangelicals' institutional resources. Evangelical scholars can probably be found in almost any leading research university, although the chances of finding them in the social sciences at such institutions are likely to be much smaller. I suspect, again without being able to prove it, that most evangelicals who are interested in bringing Christianity to bear on the human sciences are located in evangelical colleges. Simply being in a setting of this kind is likely to reinforce the concern for doing work from a Christian perspective: one's colleagues and stu-

5. Some evidence of these differences is presented in Hunter, *Evangelicalism*.

dents are likely to share the same interests, and even the official charter of the college is likely to point in this direction. In a public institution, by contrast, the sheer plurality of religious views and nonreligious views is likely to render the connection between religious values and scholarship a much more private matter.

If it is the case that most of this interest comes from evangelical colleges, one can again identify certain advantages and disadvantages. The disadvantages are clear: heavy teaching loads, a lack of graduate students, small endowments, inadequate facilities. The advantages are not inconsiderable, however: opportunities for collaborative research with like-minded colleagues and students, access to certain kinds of archives and library materials, and even a well-established circle of journals, publishing houses, and foundations. I will come back to the implications of these advantages and disadvantages.

The earlier point about networks as an influence on scholarly work also needs to be linked with these observations. Although the networks among scholars at evangelical colleges may be quite strong, I suspect that these scholars are rather poorly integrated into the dominant networks in their disciplines. Again, heavy teaching schedules, involvement in local academic and community affairs, and inadequate travel funds may be the decisive factors. But the cycle of exclusion and marginality also reinforces itself, becoming what Robert Merton in another context once termed the "Matthew effect": to those to whom much has been given, more will be given; and to those to whom little has been given, it will be taken away.[6] From going to different graduate schools or being less integrated with other graduate students, to publishing less often in mainstream journals, to developing interests not shared by the leaders of their disciplines, the cycle perpetuates itself and deepens.

Certainly, there are the exceptions: evangelical scholars who publish actively, win grants and fellowships, and maintain strong ties with scholars in secular universities. These exceptions are particularly important because they can bridge between scholars in the evangelical community and scholars outside it. But they are exceptions.

What, then, does the foregoing suggest about directions for scholarly research by evangelicals? Some will likely disagree, but I believe one should engage in research that best maximizes the resources at one's disposal, rather than simply trying to study anything and every-

6. Robert Merton, *Sociology of Science* (Chicago: University of Chicago Press, 1973), pp. 439-59.

thing that happens to be in vogue. Even at the leading research institutions one sees a high degree of specialization around the interests and resources that happen to give one department a competitive edge over another: some departments specialize in large-scale quantitative studies of status attainment, others in comparative-historical work, others in ethnomethodology, and so on. Evangelical scholars at evangelical colleges should also specialize in those topics and styles of research in which they can truly excel.

To be more specific, social scientists and the public more generally have at present an enormous interest in knowing more about evangelicals and fundamentalists, their life-styles, and their churches. This is clearly a topic on which evangelical scholars themselves should have a great deal to say, and it is one for which the resources are there.

What goes on inside a typical evangelical church? How does the pastor function? Why are these congregations growing so rapidly? Which kinds of values are affirmed in evangelical colleges? When someone converts to Christianity, what happens? Where do the students in evangelical elementary schools come from? Are these institutions different from similar ones in the past? Can evangelicalism survive the onslaught of secularism and modernization? These are questions that evangelical scholars could be (and in some cases already are) addressing.

Unlike the secular social scientist, the evangelical scholar is likely to have a great deal of intuitive, firsthand knowledge about some of these subjects already. In addition, he or she is likely to be able to gain access to individuals and organizations that others could not. Special sources of funding may even be available to evangelical scholars for such projects. Journalists and other scholars are likely to make statements about evangelical churches, often without benefit of insight or sympathy. Evangelical scholars could play a vital role, therefore, in mediating between their own domain of special understanding and the interests of the wider public.

To suggest that evangelicals study evangelicals is scarcely novel. A perusal of previous efforts of this kind in the literature, however, points out several pitfalls that need to be consciously overcome. One is a tendency to be overly apologetic; another, to speak and write only for other evangelicals; still another, to be so familiar with the subject matter that familiarity itself becomes a blinder.

It is, I suppose, for all these reasons that some of the most insightful studies of evangelicals have been done by nonevangelicals. It appears that one must gain some critical distance from one's subject matter in order to become really curious about it and ask sufficiently probing questions. For example, an anthropologist who has been conducting fieldwork in Lynchburg, Virginia, has written one of the most insightful studies of the process by which one becomes convicted by the Holy Spirit. Coming from a different religious tradition, she was able to see this process with sufficient freshness to raise some genuinely interesting questions. Had she been steeped in the Baptist tradition, she would likely have never thought to ask these questions.[7]

One answer to this dilemma is to study topics within the evangelical tradition that are at least somewhat removed from one's own background and beliefs: an ethnic church, a different denomination, a group that has a different interpretation of the Bible.[8] Another possibility is to engage in collaborative research with someone from a different tradition. Sometimes it becomes necessary to play "as if" games with one's own imagination as well. Then, at the stage of publishing, rather than being content with the evangelical press or journal closest at hand, one might find it a valuable exercise to test out one's ideas in the context of a secular press.

Among the kinds of research needed on evangelical religious expressions and institutions, one of the most necessary is in-depth ethnographic and historical research. As data sets have proliferated and evangelical colleges have come of age with the computer industry, an increasing number of evangelical scholars have turned to the analysis of public opinion surveys, comparing evangelicals with other segments of the population. Some of this research has been valuable. It has not, however, been on the cutting edge for the most part. Pollsters like George Gallup and Andrew Greeley are in a much stronger position to collect such data initially, and the typical graduate student at a leading research university is often in a better position to do the analysis with up-to-date statistical methods.

From my own perspective as a sociologist of religion, there are a number of specific areas in which evangelical sociologists might effectively focus their efforts in trying to understand the character of evangelical religion. Ethnographic research should be a high priority. We need to hear evangelical church members speaking in their own

7. My reference here is to work currently in progress by Professor Susan Harding of the University of Michigan.

8. For example, this strategy was successfully employed by George Marsden, *Fundamentalism and American Culture* (Oxford: Oxford University Press, 1980).

words to learn how they construct reality, how they confront the secular society.

I am not at all convinced that evangelicalism, or even fundamentalism, is as rigid and intolerant, as out-of-step with the times, as most intellectuals think. It may appeal to a certain simplistic, pragmatic strand in American culture, but I doubt that it is really that simplistic or unreflective.

As sociologists, we also need to learn more about the ways in which evangelical religion is organized. It may be, as most of our theories have led us to believe, that religion is primarily a matter of "demand"—of individuals expressing their needs for meaning and belonging. But we should not overlook the importance of the "supply" side of the equation either. What is it about evangelical fund-raising that makes it so effective? How are evangelical churches organized? What mechanisms have been implemented to cope with the managerial problems of congregations with thousands of members? What roles do parachurch organizations play in giving evangelicalism a nationally effective ministry? How is unity maintained at the local level?

Most of these questions can be researched best with relatively inexpensive, but perhaps labor-intensive, research strategies involving participation in local congregations and communities. Those who have behind-the-scenes access to decision-making boards and committees could provide a valuable service by making better known the importance of these bodies.

Another strategy that has been almost entirely overlooked is to focus on the discourse that goes on in these settings. For example, we need studies of sermons that show what kinds of rhetorical techniques are used, what kind of authority role for the pastor is communicated, how Scripture is handled, and how the listener is drawn into the message in a personal way. We also need studies of the informal discourse that characterizes Sunday school classes, home fellowship groups, and committee meetings.

If consensus is regarded as an important value, for example, how is a sense of consensus generated discursively? If caring and other signs of interest in personal needs are what parishioners find attractive, then what is it about these groups that conveys those expressions of community? These are simply some of the many aspects of the social life of evangelical religion that have remained unexplored.

Lest it seem that one must be a sociologist of religion to be an effective evangelical scholar, let me hasten to add that what I have suggested concerning research on evangelical churches can be extended to most other aspects of evangelical subculture. For instance, the evangelical family is an exceptionally ripe area for sociological research. Is the evangelical family withstanding the disruptive effects of secular culture, or is it too becoming victim to the pressures that lead to marital strain, divorce, and sexual experimentation? What happens when one spouse is more deeply committed to a strong evangelical faith than the other? How are changing gender roles, especially the rapid inclusion of women in the labor market, affecting the evangelical family and, in turn, the evangelical church? Similar research opportunities are present in areas such as evangelical politics, evangelicals in the workplace, evangelicals' use of leisure time, and so on.

Of course, the evangelical press and evangelical journals are filled with discussions of these topics. Journalists and theologians have been quick to seize on the popularity of these issues. Sociologists, however, can make a distinct contribution by producing the more systematic research that these impressionistic discussions often lack. And evangelical sociologists can make a valuable contribution by writing in a style and by publishing in media that communicate with readers beyond the evangelical community itself. In this sense, what I am suggesting is that evangelical sociologists can serve valuably as the interpreters of their own tradition for the broader intellectual community.

The obverse of this point suggests a second general area in which evangelical scholars can play a critical role. They can mediate the discourse of the broader academic community for their own evangelical constituencies. For example, a freshman at an evangelical college who has been reared in a deeply evangelical home and church may well not be ready to read Marx's *Theses on Feuerbach* with much understanding or appreciation. Yet it is important, I believe, for a college-educated evangelical who claims some knowledge of the human sciences to have some understanding of Marx—or Durkheim or Freud. Evangelical scholars who have studied this literature, on the one hand, but who have firsthand sensitivities of the needs and interests of evangelical students, on the other hand, can play an important role in bridging these two cultures.

Bridging this gap is one of the activities that the Institute for Advanced Christian Studies, as well as other evangelical organizations, such as the American Scientific Affiliation, have already begun to contribute to in an active way. One strategy has been to sponsor books interpreting the advances in various fields for evangelical scholars. Another has been to write textbook supplements for use in introductory classes at evangelical colleges. Still another that might be worth considering is producing teaching packets, curriculum guides, annotated bibliographies, lecture outlines, and audiovisual materials for actual classroom use.

The American Sociological Association has for some time assisted in developing such teaching materials for use in sociology courses generally. The same might be a useful strategy for materials specifically geared for use among evangelical students. In view of the demanding teaching schedules under which faculty at most evangelical colleges labor, this kind of material could also play a significant role in reducing the amount of time needed for course preparation and for updating courses.

BRIDGING THE GAP

A final area of research that I wish to emphasize specifically concerns the relations between evangelical Christians and nonevangelical or liberal Christians. Implicit in all the foregoing is the assumption that evangelical Christians are actually different in some ways from liberal Christians. Part of the argument has rested on the belief that an interest in integrating Christianity and scholarly work was more likely to come from evangelical scholars than from liberal Christian scholars. But as I have suggested in previous chapters, the difference is more pervasive. It involves a much broader cleavage in values, beliefs, and life-styles.

Not that this cleavage is all-encompassing: for example, evangelicals are much less different from the rest of the population in levels of educational attainment than they used to be. Nevertheless, there is a profound cultural gap between evangelical or conservative and liberal Christians. In addition to the fact that the two differ in their views of the Bible, in their beliefs about God, and in the kinds of churches they attend, they are also divided, as we have seen, by a high level of mutual suspicion, prejudice, and name-calling.

If one views these tensions from a purely disinterested sociological perspective, one can see that this kind of conflict sometimes has positive consequences. Liberal churches appeal to their ex-evangelical members by damning fundamentalists, and evangelical churches draw members away from the liberal churches by charging them with heresy and tepid convictions. If one views the situation from the standpoint of Christian principles, however, one can only decry the ill will, the absence of brotherly and sisterly love, and the prevalence of dogmatism and bigotry that characterize present relations between conservative and liberal Christians. Scholars on both sides who care about the Christian virtues of harmony and reconciliation could clearly take a more active role in understanding and helping to mitigate these conflicts.

Uppermost is a need for more accurate information on the beliefs and practices of Christians on both sides of the fence. I have already mentioned some of the issues that could usefully be researched among evangelicals and evangelical churches. Many of these apply to liberal churches as well.

But we must avoid the danger of trying to see liberal churches simply through the eyes of what is familiar in evangelical churches. For example, most liberal mainstream Protestant denominations in the United States have sustained serious losses in membership over the past two decades. This decline has sometimes been cause for quiet rejoicing in evangelical circles, and more often has been taken in a typically American, pragmatist style of thinking to mean that liberal beliefs must be wrong and evangelical beliefs must be right. The truth of the matter, while perhaps partly captured in this interpretation, is actually much more complex, having to do with differential fertility patterns that are in turn rooted in social class and age cohort differences, with sunk costs in facilities and changing demographic and residential trends, and with distinctive priorities and perspectives concerning missions, evangelism, the role of clergy, liturgy, and so on. Rather than simply assuming that liberal churches are dormant and uninteresting, if not overtly misguided, studies need to be done to identify areas of vitality within these congregations, to discover ministries that are not being performed elsewhere, and to learn how liberal beliefs are acted out in individual and congregational lives.

Another vital need in attempting to bridge the gap between conservative and liberal Christians is theoretical reflection. Much of this has been done by theologians, but social scientists also have valuable tools that need to be put into action. In the sociology of religion, for example, a large body of theoretical literature has been concerned with secularization, and more generally with the conflicts between traditional religion and modern culture. It would appear that some of this literature could be applied to the contemporary situation with an eye toward bringing conservative and liberal Christians closer together.

For instance, it may well be that conservative Christians have adapted more to modernity than they would like to admit, and it may be that liberal Christians have retained more of traditional Christianity than conservatives have recognized. On the issue of Christian exclusivism versus cultural pluralism, for example, both sides have struggled deeply with where to draw the line. Evangelicals have begun to view evangelism, salvation, and other world religions in ways that would have surprised their grandparents. And liberals have begun to recognize that a purely "anything goes" attitude is neither as intellectually respectable nor as organizationally desirable as their parents might have thought. Scholars could play a useful role in considering from both a theoretical and an empirical perspective what the options are on this and similar cultural dilemmas.

It should also be emphasized, as I noted at the outset of this chapter, that evangelical social scientists may be in an especially privileged situation to mediate the conflict between liberal and conservative Christians because of their own backgrounds and intellectual dispositions. Evangelical scholars—sociologists, historians, political scientists, psychologists—have often been in the forefront of liberal social and political causes within the broader evangelical community—for example, on civil rights, the Vietnam War, feminism, disarmament, sanctuary. In this way, they share some of the interests that prevail in liberal churches. They may be deeply committed to evangelical religious doctrines, but by virtue of academic training they may also be less dogmatic in dealing with others holding different views. In short, they constitute part of that vital middle ground between the two extremes. Their voice may be particularly in need of being heard as a contrast to the more shrill voices that are being exercised at those extremes.

In conclusion, one must recognize that suggesting a wish list of research topics for the intersection of evangelical Christianity and the social sciences is likely to have little consequence unless the relevant practitioners, and the editors, funding agencies, foundations, and others on whom these practitioners depend, can be motivated to pursue some of these topics. I have tried to suggest some potentially motivating considerations by placing these reflections in a broader context. To reiterate briefly, the intellectual climate in the human sciences gives respectability to interpretative, nonpositivistic kinds of research, such as that concerned with bringing Christian values to bear on scholarly topics. The intellectual community and the public at large have a tremendous interest in knowing more about evangelical Christianity. Evangelical scholars have certain institutional resources at their disposal which actually give them a competitive edge in doing certain kinds of research. A continuing need exists for evangelical scholars to mediate the broader scholarly literature in a way that evangelical readers and students can understand and appreciate. And a pressing need exists, in my view, to bring about some degree of reconciliation between evangelical Christians and liberal Christians.

The next step, I believe, would be for someone to set forth a list of testable hypotheses that could actually stimulate research and reflection in a number of concrete areas, such as religion, family, politics, gender, and so on. For that to be effective, it might best be done by individuals specializing in those particular subfields of the social sciences, or it might be valuable for it to be done collectively by groups of such specialists. If it were actually to generate research, though, it would need to be done in a daring, perhaps even contentious, manner. For example, both the strengths and the weaknesses of evangelical churches should be the subject of hypotheses. One might also generate some hypotheses about the nature of evangelical scholarship itself. Were these hypotheses contentious enough, they might well arouse the scholarly community to produce enlightening and provocative research!

Epilogue

I HAVE ARGUED THAT THE CONFLICT between religious liberals and evangelicals has become particularly intense in recent years. It has become so for a variety of reasons, not least of which are the broader societal forces to which religion in America has been exposed. These forces have torn established religious communities asunder.

Young people have fled the family farm and the local neighborhood to acquire college educations and take jobs in the professions. In the process many have adopted more liberal and relativistic views on matters of faith; some have abandoned religious communities entirely; others have returned to the fold after a season only to find it different enough to seek other havens of friendship and support.

For their part, clergy and other religious leaders have used the vast resources at their disposal to engage the society in dialogue. Some have championed the oppressed at home and abroad, waged holy wars for peace, and raised their voices in support of social justice; others have watched with alarm as moral standards seemed to slip out of the public domain and, realizing the importance of this development, seized the occasion to restore morality to the nation's conscience.

In the wider society profound social and cultural changes have contributed to the complexity of the overall climate to which laity and clergy are subject. Government takes larger and larger shares of personal income and devotes itself to many of the traditional charitable functions that churches once considered their own. The mass media have grown from a source of news and information into a major industry devoted to entertaining the leisured majority. A vast wasteland of secular hedonism has resulted, on the one hand, while new technologies have opened uncharted territories for religious broadcasting, on the other. In higher education a similar tension has arisen. Elite private colleges with a denominational heritage have increasingly been replaced by public universities. On the fringe, fundamentalist and evangelical institutions have struggled to provide an alternative more in keeping with religious tradition. All these developments have reinforced the growing division between religious liberals and religious conservatives.

If my argument is correct, the major divisions in American religion now revolve around an axis of liberalism and conservatism rather than the denominational landmarks of the past. The new division parallels the ideological cleavage that runs through American politics. It divides religious practitioners from one another over questions of social welfare, defense spending, communism, and the so-called moral politics of abortion, sex education, gender equality, and prayer in public schools. But this division is not only political; it is deeply religious as well.

Religious liberals often go out of their way to demonstrate their familiarity with historical criticisms of biblical texts; they quote their own brands of theology; and they relativize their convictions by touting the complexities of ethical decisions and the necessity of pluralism and competing viewpoints. Religious conservatives display an equally strong penchant for assertions about the truth of the Christian gospel, the authority of biblical teachings, and the dangers of undisciplined questioning of one's faith. These differences in style—both of private conviction and of public discourse—have become far more significant than the differences of doctrine and liturgy that historically pitted Presbyterians against Episcopalians and Methodists against Baptists.

The current internecine struggle between religious conservatives and liberals is not an altogether new development, however. Theological divisions have characterized American religion from the beginning. In some periods the conflict has focused on tensions between Protestants and Catholics; in others, between fundamentalists and modernists; in still others, between "Old Lights"—the adherents of traditional patterns of worship—and "New Lights"—the proponents of revivalism and popular religion.

The persistence of such divisions—changing in content, but always present in one form or another—should cause us to be curious about their functions. What role do they play? Is it only by chance that religious people seem so often to be at one another's throats? Or is conflict in some way characteristic of faith itself?

Surely the name-calling and ill will that divide evangelicals from religious liberals fall short of the ideal of Christian harmony and unity set forth in Scripture. But, living as we do in an imperfect world, we must ask whether these divisions are entirely negative. Perhaps they contribute positively to propagating the faith.

The negativity comes when strident voices respond to one another so loudly that alternative voices are simply drowned out. The voice of evangelicals and fundamentalists is perhaps heard more clearly in American society today than it was a decade or two ago. But it is doubtful that important disagreements within the conservative wing are being heard. Many spokespersons in the media, universities, and government who attempt to interpret religious conservatism are scarcely able to distinguish a fundamentalist from an evangelical, let alone sort out the varieties of eschatological teaching or doctrines of biblical inspiration that conservatives may hold. If these discussions do not find their way into public discourse, it is even more difficult for other voices—Quakers, Mormons, Brethren, Wesleyans, Adventists—to be heard. Religious pluralism is in danger of being replaced by religious polarization.

In the past, denominational structures and local congregations provided containers for religious divisions that often prevented them from getting out of hand. The folks at First Baptist might be fighting each other tooth and nail, but the feud was at least unlikely to enlist the help of the Congregationalists across town. Organizational procedures, the parliamentary rules governing church politics, and the charismatic authority of strong preachers could usually keep doctrinal conflicts within limits.

Nowadays, the problem is aggravated by national media, both secular and religious. The secular media love nothing more than to print stories about clergy defying their denominations or to heighten the intensity of "talk show realism" by staging a shouting match between a rabid atheist and an equally rabid fundamentalist.

The tendency toward religious polarization is also aggravated by the erosion of denominational boundaries. When these boundaries were strong, public debate required representatives of all the major denominations and faiths to play an active role. For the annual Memorial Day services in most communities, at least one rabbi, one Roman Catholic priest, and one pastor from the Protestant council of clergy were invited. For more serious business, such as that conducted by the local ministerial council or by various national federations, the etiquette of denominational representation was also well understood. It was indeed a matter of symbolism and protocol, but it ensured the representation of multiple voices.

Some time ago I wrote about a development in American society which I called "religious populism." It was comparable in religious circles to what social analysts saw happening in modern societies more generally. With the extension of mass media and a breakdown of institutional authority, people were becoming undifferentiated consumers—inhabitants of the proverbial "mass society." At the grass roots, this development meant that people increasingly chose their own private forms of religious expression rather than relying on the authority of a tradition or a religious community. Equally significant was a tendency for leaders to lose important protections from the pressures brought to bear on them by their constituencies. Rather than being able to draw on the authority of their office, their calling, or even their specialized knowledge, clergy were thrust into the harsh glare of public criticism. They had to play to the media, fill large auditoriums, and speak the words that seemed most relevant at the moment. The result was that meeker souls lost out.

The present conflict in American religion can be understood as one of the inevitable consequences of religious populism. The erosion of denominational authority, together with the rising influence of the mass media, have subjected clergy and laity alike to the standards of popular taste. Only the champions of large constituencies on the left or the right can be heard.

Much of the conflict currently evident in American religion still takes place within the local church, though. It is not simply the product of religious television or of political controversies in the wider society. If it reflects these broader currents, it is nevertheless reinforced from the pulpit. Clergy in liberal churches denounce fundamentalists and evangelicals. Clergy in conservative churches lash out against the paganism of their liberal counterparts. Often it would be just as effective to remain quiet. Thus, we must ask ourselves why clergy bother to levy these barrages from the pulpit and why parishioners seem so willing to listen.

It has been said that every form of discourse evokes counterdiscourse. At the simplest level, we define things by their opposites:

white by black, good by bad. In more complex ways we always speak with an implicit negative providing the background for what we say. Our talk of the United States is set implicitly within the context of our negative assumptions about the Soviet Union. We even develop our self-concepts by making implicit comparisons between ourselves and others. It is not surprising, therefore, to find discourse and counter-discourse in American religion.

Indeed, Scripture itself provides plenty of precedent for identifying one's position by expressing negative comments about other positions. Consider what happened when the rich young ruler came to Jesus for instruction. Jesus could have engaged in a dialogue involving only two parties: himself, the religious leader; and the ruler, not exactly a worldly person but at least a representative of the culture of his day. The parable Jesus told might have been much simpler: a man, representing mankind in its descent from Jerusalem to Jericho, was beaten and robbed; a good man, the Samaritan, came along and helped him; go and do thou likewise. Instead, the parable is more complex. Much of its interest hinges on the fact that Jesus has two other characters pass by the injured man without stopping to help him. These characters are representatives of religion. They provide contrasts, not simply between the religious and the secular, but between two varieties of religion itself.

In our own context, defining ourselves as religious conservatives by saying negative things about religious liberals is partly done for the sake of convenience. Religious competitors know the same stories and speak the same language. A member of the clergy who castigates another religious point of view may well speak from experience. It is a view he himself has held at some point. Or he has been exposed to it at Thursday morning's meeting of the ministerial council. It may be a view held by some of the members of his own church.

In addition to its convenience, there may be a variety of other reasons why religious discourse is framed in terms of invectives against other religious viewpoints. The enemy within may be more real and dangerous than the enemy without. The liberal pastor who decries fundamentalism from the pulpit may have been visited the night before by conservatives from his congregation. He is less likely to have been visited by secular humanists trying to convince him to abandon his faith entirely. Discourse oriented toward religious competitors also keeps things in-house, as it were. Clergy may know something about competing theological visions; they may not be in a position to speak with authority about the latest developments in the secular world.

Beyond this, preaching to the converted allows one to start with common assumptions, with an audience that shares some common ground, and then try to move that audience toward a particular commitment.

In short, the conflict between religious liberals and conservatives may perform a variety of positive functions. It helps each side define its own positions more clearly. It keeps the focus on religious teachings themselves—and even when these teachings are disputed, they are the focus of discourse, rather than being replaced by talk about secular topics. The two sides may even imitate one another and learn from one another. Liberals might not want to admit it, but seeing the conservative church down the road growing rapidly may encourage them to start Bible studies and youth programs. Conservatives might be equally reluctant to admit it, but witnessing the influence of liberals in Washington, or the efforts of liberals to help the poor, may set their own efforts in motion in a similar direction.

To pursue this line of argument to its logical conclusion would suggest that the conflict between religious liberals and conservatives may not be that serious after all. It is perhaps only polite posturing, the loving good-natured bantering of two siblings. It is a dialogue that keeps things lively, but one that exists symbiotically. An occasional barb hurled at the other side is no cause for alarm.

One can extend this interpretation further. Viewed as a symbiotic relationship, the conflict between conservatives and liberals may be seen as a genuine benefit to both, rather than an "I win—you lose" struggle for the United States. The interpretation advanced by many analysts of American religion may be wrong: perhaps the main dynamic is not evangelical growth and liberal decline. Instead, the two factions may be supporting each other. Thus, the strength of American evangelicalism is partly attributable to the viable liberal theology in relation to which evangelicalism can define itself. And religious liberalism might be even weaker were it not for the strength of American evangelicalism.

This interpretation has considerable merit. The growth of fundamentalism as a distinct movement early in the century was certainly made possible by a clearly delineated modernist movement against which fundamentalism could define itself. The evangelical movement that grew during the 1950s and 1960s was also able to define itself as an alternative to religious liberalism. For those who disdained the liberal churches' involvement in civil rights and antiwar protests, the personal piety of evangelicalism provided a nonpoliticized alternative. For those who could no longer understand the complex theological views being expressed in liberal churches, evangelicalism provided the rock-solid security of biblical authority and the historical Jesus. Many who have switched into evangelical churches have in fact come from the more liberal mainstream.

At the same time, religious liberalism has defined itself as an alternative to naive fundamentalism, apparently much more so even than as an alternative to brash secular humanism. Theological liberalism presented itself traditionally as a perspective more in keeping with science and higher education—indeed, with progress in general—than the rigid beliefs of its benighted kinfolk in fundamentalist churches. In more recent years this naive faith in social progress has broken down. But religious liberalism continues to pose as a more sophisticated alternative to evangelicalism. Fundamentalists and evangelicals do have simple answers, liberals will argue, but their answers are too simplistic. What mature person can believe them? They do not work in the real struggles of life. One needs to move beyond them, particularly as one gains exposure to higher education or as one confronts genuine crises. Faith, it is argued, should be a developmental process. One may start out at a low level characterized by the black-and-white answers of fundamentalism, but then one must advance toward higher stages of faith that include the more complex cognitive styles of the religious liberal.

From this point of view, the present woes of the liberal mainstream denominations are more a matter of demographics (low birth rates), geographic mobility (especially among the young), and sunk costs (often in declining neighborhoods) than it is of anything basically wrong with their teachings. The liberal churches should not abandon their views and become more like evangelicals. They should continue what they are already doing, perhaps only modifying their programs to make them more effective. They should in fact provide an alternative to fundamentalism. They should combat dogmatism and overly narrow views of biblical ethics. They should champion the openness, the expansiveness, the mystery of the Christian gospel. They should appeal to the life of the mind with theology and literature and liturgy, rather than emulating the mass hysteria of the television preachers.

Evangelicals should also continue to present themselves as an alternative to religious liberalism. They should not grow soft on evangelism and complacent about missionary programs. They should not follow the liberal churches down paths of accommodation with secularism on important questions of theology and morality. They should recognize the strength within their own heritage. They should recount the biblical narratives in ways that make them meaningful to today's world. They should continue to challenge liberalism when it becomes indulgent in its own intellectual pretensions.

Tension of this kind between evangelicals and liberals is likely for the most part to strengthen the overall place of religion in American society. The limitation comes when neither side questions the deeper assumptions on which its position rests, or challenges the secular culture. At a recent forum sponsored by a large liberal church, a seminary professor with much erudition and experience stood up to put in a good word, as he saw it, for evangelicals. One must try to understand them, he cautioned, because they are simply products of their culture. If they focus on individual piety and if they listen to the sleek broadcasts of wealthy television preachers, it is only because of the individualism and materialism in our culture more generally. His argument was sensitive to the differences in American religion and undoubtedly worth considering seriously. Yet, as I listened, I wondered if he was aware that the assumptions of his own liberal theology were also reflections of the culture to which he was exposed.

Evangelicals and liberals alike are products to some extent of the distinctive place they occupy in American culture. Each has developed a set of assumptions and a style of discourse with which its constituency feels comfortable. Evangelical preachers show off their familiarity with obscure passages of the Bible; liberal preachers, their schooling in historical criticism. One side argues that the Christian message is very simple; the other, that its meaning is more complex than meets the eye. One insists it wants "only the facts, ma'am," while the other goes out of its way to show that it really does not believe the literal or historical truth of the facts reported. One makes a virtue of questioning nothing; the other, a virtue of questioning everything.

The contrasts in style are clear. Each can see how the other deviates from its own standards. But the lens of criticism also needs to be turned inward. Both need to ask why they have chosen to cherish some assumptions and to reject others. Both need to be aware of the larger cultural forces to which they are subject. The forces of rationality, efficiency, material success, and self-sufficiency are all particularly strong in our culture. They hammer away incessantly at the doors of religious faith. Their blows are reinforced by the power of the secular media, the universities, the marketplace, and the government. Evangelicals and liberals alike need to pay heed to the effects of these blows.

The conflict between evangelicals and liberals is also unhealthy when it simply polarizes opinion. Religious discourse fails to advance when conflict causes communication to break down. When liberals charge conservatives with bigotry, dogmatism, and fundamentalist rigidity, never pausing to examine the tolerance and complexity of conservative thought, they succumb to this danger. When evangelicals accuse liberals of paganism, heresy, and untruth, they also polarize opinion to the point that liberals' commitment to the same God and the same religious heritage is overlooked. Certainly the important issues cannot be joined in serious dialogue when a particularly unpopular television preacher is taken to represent all of one side while a radically relativistic member of the clergy who tolerates everything and stands for nothing is regarded as a spokesperson for the other.

Of course, much has been said in religious circles about the need for dialogue. Typically this call was for greater interaction among representatives of different denominations. The same need is now urgently present for dialogue between religious conservatives and liberals. Local congregations need to create opportunities for each side to express its views and hear the views of the other side. Similar dialogues need to take place in religious periodicals, on religious television programs, in gatherings of clergy, and at theological seminaries.

In addition, discourse about discourse is needed. Like the discussion at Princeton University to which I made reference in the Prologue, we need occasions that help us try to understand better the assumptions we make about discourse itself. We need to consider the ways in which rhetorical styles may inhibit open discussion. We need to examine more carefully the buzz words that may define us as insiders and others as outsiders. We need to understand the rules implicit in discourse so that we know better when to apply them and when to violate them. Some occasions clearly require a simple declarative statement. Others need to permit expressions of personal sentiment and emotion. Still others warrant frank disagreements.

Consensus may not always be the objective of such dialogue. Religious conservatives and liberals have legitimate differences of opinion. These differences need not be run through the blender of debate to create some gruel that neither side finds palatable. Ways of maintaining and encouraging respect for diversity need to be set up. At the same time, there may indeed be common ground worthy of exploration.

There is also value in developing a stronger middle-of-the-road position as a distinct alternative to both the extreme right and the extreme left. Liberal evangelicalism (or evangelical liberalism) is an important option to cultivate. A position of this kind would reject both the authoritarianism of the right and the extreme relativism of the left. It would assert the distinctive significance of biblical faith and yet recognize the role of interpretation in understanding and applying that faith. It would reject the purely naturalistic faith of a secular worldview, insisting on the ultimacy of divine grace, and yet resist those claiming to have an absolute corner on the expression of this truth. Occupying its own distinctive cultural space within American religion, it would also provide a place for the creative joining together and rethinking of social and moral issues, such as abortion, nuclear disarmament, stewardship, and social justice.

In sum, there is a role to be played in American religion by the polarized flanks from which so much has been heard in recent years and an equally important role to be played by alternative positions closer to the middle. The work at the poles is to define the issues in terms of clear oppositions. These oppositions set the outer limits of debate and they unmask any false consensus that may inhibit an honest rethinking of public values. The work at the center—the difficult work that must take place in community—is to bring these choices together in faithful and creative ways.

Index

Abortion, 36, 44-45, 80
American Civil Liberties Union (ACLU), ix, xii
Antiwar movement. *See* Vietnam War
Atheism, 26

Baptists, 71, 73
Bible: reading, 49; sales of, 50; views of, 23, 28
Bureaucracy. *See* Government; Welfare state

Capitalism, 14
Christian colleges, 158-76
Christians, and Jews, 32
Church and state issues, 58-59
Church attendance, 47, 146-47
Church membership, 109-14
Churches, 28-29, 81-84, 109
Cities. *See* Urbanization
Civil privatism, 97-114

Civil rights movement, 16, 33
Civil War, 19-21
Clergy, 50, 86, 181-82
Colleges and universities. *See* Education
Community, 10, 100-101, 118, 132-33, 180
Confession. *See* Morality
Conflict, religious, 17, 21-26, 42-44, 78-79, 140-41, 178-79
Congregations. *See* Churches
Conservatism. *See* Religious right
Constitution. *See* First Amendment

Denominationalism, 24, 27-28, 72

Economy, 8, 29
Ecumenism, 27, 53
Education: and denominational switching, 86; expansion of, 61, 106; higher, and religion, xiv,

34-35, 77; and religious television viewing, 139
Elders, Presbyterian, 86-87
Episcopalians, 73
Ethnic groups, 105
Evangelicals, 17, 35, 48, 138, 158, 166-73, 183-84

Feminism, 60, 86-87
First Amendment, 40, 55-57
Free expression. *See* First Amendment
Fundamentalists, 22, 42, 48-49, 70, 182

Government, 4, 6, 102

Humanism. *See* Secular humanism

Idolatry, 130
Imagination. *See* Religious imagination
Individualism, 4, 117, 133
Institute for Advanced Christian Studies, 172

Leaders. *See* Clergy; Elders; Television evangelists
Liberals, religious, 17, 22, 42, 78-79, 182-83
Lutherans, 71, 73, 75

Market sector. *See* Economy
Mass media, 25, 115-41
Methodists, 71, 73
Modernism, 70
Morality, 134-35, 139

Narcissism. *See* Individualism

Nonprofit sector. *See* Voluntary associations
Novels, 130
Nuclear weapons, 30, 91

Politics, and religion, 54
Prayer, and public schools, 42
Presbyterianism, 68-94
Privatism. *See* Civil privatism
Protestants, and Catholics, 32, 39, 74
Public sphere, 10-14, 30, 66, 107
Puritanism, 149

Race relations. *See* Civil rights movement
Reformation, Protestant, 129-30
Religion, views of in public opinion, 47-48
Religious conflict. *See* Conflict, religious
Religious expression. *See* First Amendment
Religious imagination, 129-32
Religious pluralism, 16
Religious right, ix-x, 121
Revivalism, 123
Right. *See* Religious right

Schisms, 70-71
Schools. *See* Education
Science, 26, 142-57
Secular humanism, 43, 153-56
Secularization, 15
Social classes. *See* Education
Social sciences. *See* Science
Supreme Court. *See* U.S. Supreme Court

Television evangelists, 22, 49, 62, 115-41

Third sector. *See* Voluntary associations

Universities. *See* Education
Urbanization, 104
U.S. Supreme Court, 55-57

Values. *See* Public sphere

Vietnam War, 33-34
Voluntary associations, 3-4, 9-14,
  99-100
Voting, 102

Welfare state, 13-14, 97-114
Women, ordination of, 79, 86

"Average age of my congregation is dead"